COMPOSING A SUCCESSFUL APPLICATION ESSAY

Write Your Way Into College

George Ehrenhaft

BARRON'S

New York • London • Toronto • Sydney

All inquiries should be addressed to:
Barron's Educational Series, Inc.
250 Wireless Boulevard
Hauppauge, New York 11788

Library of Congress No. 87-13905
International Standard Book No. 0-8120-2997-6

Library of Congress Cataloging-in-Publication Data

Ehrenhaft, George.
    Write you way into college: Composing a successful application essay

    Includes index.
    1. College applications.   2. Exposition (Rhetoric)
3. Universities and colleges — Admissions. I. Title.
LB2351.5.E37   1987   378'.1057   87-13905
ISBN 0-8120-2997-6

PRINTED IN THE UNITED STATES OF AMERICA
789   500   987654321

For Dave, Ellie, and Sylvia

Every college and university should ask prospective students to submit an essay as part of their application for admission not only to underline the importance of writing but also as a means of learning more about the needs as well as the strengths of students.

          – A recommendation from
             College: The Undergraduate
             Experience in America, a 1986 study of
             education by the Carnegie Foundation for
             the Advancement of Teaching

Table of Contents

ACKNOWLEDGMENTS

Scores of people have contributed to this book. Many are the high school students who populated my English classes during the last 20 years. They taught *me*, I believe, far more than I could ever have taught them about the craft of writing. From their stumbling but sincere writing efforts, I learned what it takes to make words clear, interesting and correct. The lessons they taught me echo through these pages.

A college application essay offers a writing teacher the ultimate high. Perhaps for the first time, students write something that counts for more than just a grade in school. They see that skill in writing can make a difference in their lives, that words empower them to disturb the universe. For showing me the way, I'm indebted to Rose Scotch, Michael DiGennaro and Susan Freeman.

I'm also grateful to the dozens of students who consented to have their college essays reproduced—in whole or in part—throughout this volume. Most of the essays were written in Mamaroneck (New York) High School, but they come, too, from Scarsdale, White Plains, John Jay and Berkshire School.

The gracious volunteers in Mamaroneck's College Information Center gave expert help and provided a site for fruitful discussions with college admissions representatives from across the nation. Also, along the road to publication, Don Reis's guiding hand kept me from stumbling.

I save my biggest hug for Al Greenberg. As Al talked to me about writing application essays, I realized that he probably should have written this book. In a sense, I became another of the countless students who have benefited from his insights and experience as a counselor.

Also, to Susan, your support has been incalculable.

G.E.

1 YOUR ESSAY MAKES A DIFFERENCE

Step into a fantasy for a moment, and sit at the desk of a college admissions officer reviewing applications for next year's freshman class. Better still, play the role yourself. You've read about forty-five applications today, and you are down to your last three. Your colleagues have gone home. It's dark outside, and you are tired and hungry. The stack of rejected applications on your desk reaches almost to the level of your aching eyes. The "maybe" pile is half as tall. A wire basket marked "yes!" holds another stack barely 3 inches high.

At eight o'clock tomorrow the admissions committee will need your decision. Each applicant comes from a good high school. Teachers and counselors have sent warm endorsements. None of the three has alumni connections—they'll sink or swim on their own. What will you recommend? Admit? Wait-list? Reject?

Jeff G's papers show you that he has taken tough courses in high school and that he will graduate in the top 10 percent of his class. You also note SAT scores near 600 in both verbal and math and participation in school life as a yearbook staffer, cross-country runner and cocaptain of the debate team. Then you come to the essay question, which asks applicants to describe an important personal experience and explain its significance. Jeff's response is rather uninspired. It makes the point that involvement in various high school activities has taught him to be a serious-minded, hard-working and responsible person. In college he expects to study hard and earn good grades.

Kathy E's application boasts several achievements in foreign languages. You observe that Kathy has won school certificates in Spanish and French and that she has also studied German. She plans to major in languages and hopes someday to work for the U.S. Department of State. Her overall average is 90 and her verbal SAT score is 630. In school she joined the language clubs and helped to publish a foreign language newspaper. Her essay contains a list of European countries she visited during the last two summers and makes the point that, although travel is broadening and fun, there's no place like home.

Pat McM's application shows that he earned an 86 average in a generally rigorous academic program, including an AP history course. Scores on SAT and achievements are not distinguished, but still within the range for your college. Pat acted in high school drama productions, played trumpet in the jazz band and in eleventh grade devoted considerable time to Students for Peace. To answer the essay question, he wrote an imaginary conversation with God after the earth had been demolished in a nuclear war.

These are three good students, three qualified candidates for admission to your college. A high average and varied activities strengthen Jeff's application. Kathy's special interest in language commends her strongly. Pat's commitment to outside activities compensates for his marginal numbers. Which of them would you accept?

How Colleges Decide

"The quality of the academic program—the content of the student's courses throughout secondary school—will be the first thing admissions officers look for," says Edward Wall, Amherst's dean of admissions.

After checking your grades and courses, each college will take a slightly different path. Some turn to your recommendations from counselors and teachers, others to test results. Although nearly all colleges tell you to take SATs or ACTs, they don't all give the scores equal weight.

You won't spring to life for the admissions committee without a thoughtful, well-written essay.

How you spent time outside of class is crucial, too, because colleges seek people who have charged full speed ahead into life. They want students who will participate, who will help shape the life on campus or in the community. They judge you according to the depth of your involvement, not by the number of activities you've joined.

The reputation of your secondary school may also count. Colleges know the schools that habitually send out high-achieving, energetic learners. In addition, colleges like a geographic blend, often favoring candidates from distant regions of the country.

An alumni connection often helps, and a congenial interview

also adds strength to your record, especially when you travel to the campus to meet an admissions official in person.

Each section of a college application adds another piece to your portrait. You won't spring to life for the admissions committee, though, without a thoughtful, well-written essay. The essay is a window into your mind and personality: Unlike an A in chemistry or a B+ in English, it reveals your uniqueness—what you think about, what drives you, and to what you aspire. Of course, it demonstrates your writing ability, too. The gift of saying what you want to say the way you want to say it can compensate for a weakness in almost any other part of the application. Typically, an effective essay can go a long way to offset a flawed SAT score. In fact, if most applicants poured as much sweat into their essays as they do into SAT preparation, admissions officials would be inundated with volumes of first-rate reading.

The needs of the college

Although colleges use different screening procedures, their intent is always the same—to choose a mix of bright, confident and positive people who will help to make the college a stimulating place for the next 4 years. "There's no such thing as an ideal candidate," says Darlene Brinker of Stanford. "Rather, we try to pick an ideal class." Since the mix keeps changing, a person in this year's freshman class might not have been accepted a year later.

Colleges want a mix of bright, confident and positive people.

A college's needs vary. From time to time a college will search specifically for debaters, high-divers, cartoonists, dancers—in short, any students blessed with a particular talent at present in short supply on the campus. If most of the drummers in a college's marching band are seniors, for example, you can bet that admissions people are keeping a sharp lookout for academically qualified high school drummers.

Your chances of being accepted depend also on the number of people seeking admission that year. Interest in a college rises and falls, sometimes with the fortunes of its athletic teams. When Villanova won a national basketball title, applications jumped 25 percent. The University of Virginia got 2000 additional applicants after basketball star Ralph Sampson announced that he wouldn't turn professional until he graduated because the education at UVA was too good to give up. At the same time, bad news depresses the number of applications. During the Vietnam War, the West Point admissions office was much quieter than it is today. Student unrest and strikes sometimes lead to fluctuating enrollment figures. Columbia officials worry whenever a murder in the streets of New York receives wide media coverage.

Applications to Smith, Holyoke and Wellesley—all prestigious women's colleges—fell off during the years when similar schools like Vassar, Sarah Lawrence and Connecticut College opened their doors to men. Even widely read college reference books can influence the ebb and flow of applications. Georgetown, for instance, got a lift when Barron's *Profiles of American Colleges* reclassified the college from "highly competitive" to "most competitive," the equivalent of adding a fourth star to a three-star rating.

The admissions committee at work

Accept? Wait-list? Reject? Thousands of decisions every year—each made thoughtfully and humanely, with complete awareness that a concerned applicant is waiting for a verdict.

What would you tell Jeff, Kathy and Pat? The majority of colleges in the United States would probably admit all three without hesitation, glad to have attracted applicants of such high caliber. But the most selective schools, the so-called "hot" colleges, would screen them with agonizing care before deciding. An admissions committee may assign numerical ratings to each candidate's academic and personal qualities. Two committee members may read each folder and make a recommendation. Difficult folders may be passed around the committee for a group decision.

Only 175 of nearly 2000 colleges in the U.S. receive three or more applications for each place in the freshman class.

Perhaps only 175 of nearly 2000 four-year colleges in the United States receive three, four, five, six or even more applications for each place in the freshman class. In 1986, highly competitive Wesleyan, for instance, accepted just 1714 of 4356 applicants. The Air Force Academy took 1765 of 7945. Yale accepted 2182 of 11,737, and Stanford accepted only 2507 of its 17,652 applicants, about a 1:7 ratio. Although the numbers differ, the admissions picture is similar at selective schools all across the country.

Even at colleges where the competition isn't quite as hot, admissions people take pains to assemble a varied and qualified student body. A few colleges, struggling to stay in business, admit virtually anyone who applies, and others, bound by law, employ open admissions. Such schools are the exception. As a rule, selectivity is practiced everywhere, and the screening of applicants is never done haphazardly.

Colleges immediately eliminate anyone who can't do the work. At the University of Pennsylvania, "85 percent of our applicants are academically qualified," says admissions dean Marie M. Kent, which means that more than 11,000 of Penn's 13,000 applicants survive the first cut. Next, a college may pick out a small group of superstars, from Presidential Scholars to world-class swimmers. The balance of the candidates are left in what Harry Bauld, an ex-admissions representative at Brown and Columbia, terms "the gray area." These applicants, Bauld says, are "in the ball park" but still far from being accepted. Faced with large numbers of good scholastic records—like those submitted by Jeff, Kathy and Pat—admissions officials make decisions using what Kent calls the "intangibles," qualities that don't show up on a transcript and can't be listed in a résumé. In particular, many colleges rely heavily on application essays.

The Application Essay

The essay can make or break an application," says Barry Taylor, who reads candidates' essays in the Tufts University admissions office. At Williams three admissions people read every essay. At Stanford, four or five admissions people sometimes read an essay before the applicant is accepted. "It's *that* important," according to Darlene Brinker, an admissions representative.

"The essay can make or break an application," says Tufts University.

Brinker also asserts that the essay is the "wild card" in the application, the piece that could give an edge to a student like Pat McM. Writing a conversation with God shows that Pat has the courage to take intellectual and creative risks. Pat's approach is unique, and it confirms his interest in issues of war and peace. That he wrote a dialogue may suggest that his drama experience has left an enduring mark on the way he thinks. In short, he put himself into his writing.

On the other hand, Jeff G and Kathy E wrote proper, but boring, essays, which couldn't be distinguished from hundreds of others. Jeff's "what-I-did-in-high-school-and-what-I-learned-from-it" approach is common and uninspired, and so is Kathy's conclusion. Kathy roamed Europe but brought back a cliché. By submitting dull essays, both Jeff and Kathy have tarnished otherwise sterling records and have jeopardized their chances of getting into a selective college.

Laura Gordon, Harvard's admissions head, believes that the essay provides "an opportunity for the students to project themselves." Students can reveal their uniqueness in an essay; they can show their personalities, reflect on their lives, display their creativity, tell the college what makes them tick. It's the only place on the college application form where students don't have to be serious, where they can have some fun.

Fun is serious business in college admissions. No, it's not a constant party inside the admissions offices at Johns Hopkins, Northwestern and Duke. These are a few of the schools, though, that frequently revise their application forms to inspire more interesting essays. Stanford changes its questions every year. Essay readers want to enjoy their work, and they do a better job if each batch of essays responds to a fresh question. Also, each class takes on an identity. Members of Dartmouth's class of 1990 faced a "greatest challenge" essay—presumably not the essay itself. Applicants for the class of 1991 had to invent their own question and answer it. Admissions people at Penn realized that by asking the same old questions they got the same old answers. They recently replaced a conventional "definition of success" question with a more sprightly one: "You've just written a 300-page autobiography; please submit page 217 with this application."

At colleges with less rigorous admissions standards, officials also read application essays attentively. Like their associates at the hottest colleges, they seek the best, most promising and vibrant students they can find. Although the essays may not always count as heavily in admissions decisions, officials sometimes use writing samples to place students in the proper academic program. Furthermore, the essays help colleges see each applicant more clearly and personally. For example, an essay may explain why a bright student earned mediocre grades in high school, or it may reveal how a family or financial problem prevented an applicant from participating in school or community activities. In addition, a college official can often tell from an essay whether the applicant may be eligible for a restricted scholarship or other type of special aid. Eventually, essays wind up in the college files. Sometimes teachers, administrators and counselors turn to application essays for helpful background information about their students.

Still, colleges of all stripes are most impressed by a student's academic performance. A perfect essay—even if such a thing existed—doesn't make up for mediocre grades or a transcript full of snap courses. Yet, nothing on the application wields as much power as a forceful essay. Poignant personal stories have pushed admissions committees to the verge of tears. But you can bet that no admissions officer has ever wept over an applicant's list of part-time jobs.

Write your way into college

A 1986 Carnegie Foundation study found that America's most selective colleges choose students by their grades, their activities and their *ability to write the application essay!* Nevertheless, no more than a third of all applicants seem to work very hard on their essays. According to Cornell admissions officials, a majority of applicants still think that good grades, test scores and recommendations will unlock the college gates for them. They send in muddled essays, not realizing that, by giving the essay all they've got, they might actually write their way into college.

> **By giving the essay all you've got, you could actually write your way into college.**

The essay hasn't always borne such weight. High-school counselors Alfred Greenberg and John O'Brien found in a survey 10 years ago that most highly selective colleges ranked the essay no higher than seventh or eighth among a dozen admissions criteria. At the time, Georgetown's dean of admissions explained why: "Some of our most able candidates can't seem to write a decent paragraph. If we were to judge students on their writing alone, we'd turn away half of our strongest candidates." Since then the writing has improved. Starting in the late 1970s the teaching of writing became a priority in schools everywhere. Today's high school juniors and seniors have received far more writing instruction than their older brothers and sisters. They write better, too, according to the National Assessment of Educational Progress, which periodically evaluates the writing of 17-year-olds across the country.

As students began to write better, colleges started asking them to write more. For some schools, such as Syracuse and the University of Southern California, you must write two or three short pieces in addition to one main essay. Boston University asks for two essays, each between 250 and 500 words. Both Swarthmore and Bennington want three pieces of writing. Barnard's applicants must write a personal statement and ten paragraphs, each responding to a different question. Some colleges tell applicants to submit not only an essay but a paper written for a high school course, complete with teacher comments and grade.

In the future, the increased demand for writing is likely to continue. The highly respected Carnegie Foundation recommends that "*every* college and university should ask prospective students to submit an essay as part of their application," not only to underscore the importance of writing, but to learn more about the strengths and weaknesses of the students. If half of an incoming class submits essays without a focus or lacking in detail, for example, the college knows exactly what it ought to be teaching in its freshman writing courses.

Although the nation's choosiest colleges ask prospective students for writing samples, many of the less competitive colleges don't—

sometimes because they don't have the staff to read them. State universities, like those in Connecticut, Minnesota, New Hampshire and Wisconsin, for instance, don't require essays. The University of Virginia, though, with 12,000 applicants a year, does. At the University of California in Berkeley, a large team of people reads the annual flood of 17,000 applications. At Stanford, Penn and other private universities, the faculty often joins admissions personnel in marathon reading sessions.

At every college that requires an essay, you can depend on one thing: essays are read thoughtfully. At Bennington, Bryn Mawr and Smith, where the essay carries as much weight as any other part of the application, committees discuss applicants' writing at length. When admissions people convene for all-day sessions at Wesleyan, they guard against careless reading by taking frequent breaks. An application that surfaces late in the afternoon is read as respectfully as one at nine o'clock in the morning.

Although finding your way into the right college may seem like traversing a labyrinth, hundreds of thousands of students make the

In your essay, show the admissions staff you're too good to turn down.

trip every year. At times the admissions system may appear fickle and unpredictable, almost beyond understanding. Yet, it works. As a college-bound student, you took your first steps toward your destination years ago when you learned to read and write and to compute numbers. You've studied, worked and contributed in some way to your school and community. You've taken college boards or ACTs and established your school record. You narrowed your college preferences, and perhaps had an interview or two.

By the time you fill in your name on your first application, the facts about you—for better or worse—are in. You can't change them. The opportunities in your essay are wide open, however. In your answers to the essay questions you have the chance to sparkle, to show the admissions staff that you're too good to turn down. Let the essay work for you. The remainder of this book will help you do it.

2 ESSAYS THAT WORK

In a survey about "life's ten most anxious moments," a majority of high school seniors agreed that getting up to talk in front of a group provoked the most anxiety. Second was applying to college, especially writing the essay.

It's easy to see why. The two tasks—addressing a group and composing an essay for a college application—have a lot in common. In both cases success depends on how well you present yourself, what you have to say and how effectively you convey your message. Few people don't feel at least a little stage fright before facing an audience, and it's equally natural to feel edgy about filling up an empty sheet of paper with an essay that could clear or block your entry to your college of choice.

Success depends on how well you present yourself, what you have to say and how effectively you convey your message.

In a letter to all prospective applicants to Sarah Lawrence College, director of admissions Deborah J. Wright says, "Take a deep breath, relax and believe in yourself." The advice is good, but hard to follow when all at the same time you're applying to several colleges (each demanding a different essay), you're trying to keep your grades up and you're finding every week just too darn short!

Annette R, a high school senior interested in St. Lawrence University, dealt with the pressure by trying to guess what the admissions office would expect her to write in response to the charge, "Describe a significant experience or achievement that has special meaning for you." She searched the college catalogue for a clue to what the college might like and landed on this statement: "We seek candidates who demonstrate a willingness to take an interest in the lives and welfare of others." OK, she concluded, if they like social do-gooders, I'll give them a social do-gooder. So she set out to prove that she and St. Lawrence were meant for each other. She began her essay,

In your brochure you said that you like candidates who are interested in the lives of others. I would like to attend St. Lawrence because that description fits me perfectly. I am the type of person who likes people. I have many friends that I love dearly. I cannot walk the hallways of the high school without saying hello to someone. I am very happy that I have so many friends, and feel that I have so many because of my job. My job helps me to relate to people.

The balance of the essay described her job as a receptionist in a dentist's office, where she often comforted people with aching jaws.

Annette had the academic credentials for St. Lawrence, but was rejected. She had made the fatal mistake of trying to guess what she thought the college wanted, an approach always filled with peril. Admissions people don't want anything in particular except to have applicants write something that accurately portrays themselves. There are no hidden answers to the questions. Applicants "shouldn't try to figure out what a school is looking for," says Harvard's admissions dean Laura Gordon Fisher. "They should just be themselves."

Annette made the mistake of trying to guess what the college wanted.

Write Honestly About Yourself

In an essay about a "rewarding experience," Susan E gave Yale an honest self-portrait. She wrote about her audition for a summer school in the arts. The tryouts, Susan said, were not unlike writing a college essay:

> Acting is, after all, the art of revealing character, and that is what I am trying to do now: present a clear picture of Susan E's character . . . so, if you don't mind, I'm going to think of this whole affair as an audition.
>
> Actually, my experience with acting auditions is very limited. The most memorable and important audition I have ever had was for a summer theater program that I attended after my junior year. There were two auditions, a semifinal and a final round, and each time I performed two dramatic monologues. I created other people's characters and spoke other people's words. Thinking back on the experience, I believe my own character and my own words would have been infinitely more interesting. . . .

Susan then quoted the monologue she recited and describes what she felt after the audition:

> There's the tremendous feeling of accomplishment. I suppose that's a big part of it—the accomplishment. I don't

imagine performing would stimulate me so much if I had no success at it. In fact, if I were lousy at it, I probably would stay clear of it as much as possible—like gym. . . . Yeah, failure generally stinks. It's very scary to fail. In fact, right about now I'm going to start the seemingly unending process of contemplating this audition. "Did it go well? Did I say too much? Was I too honest? Did I sound silly? Will they laugh about this for weeks to come?"—Paranoia strikes deep, but fear of failure strikes deeper. Then I'll go the other way: "Of course they liked you. Honesty is refreshing. It took guts to be silly and they'll respect you for it." Well, I guess I'll know soon enough.

There's more, but by now you must have noticed that there's an honest-to-goodness person writing the words here. Susan's essay could be an entry in her diary—it's that personal.

Write About Something Important to You

Colleges ask for an essay largely because they want to get to know you. When the admissions staff has finished your essay, they should have a vivid sense of your personality. If you give them only what you think they want, you're being dishonest, posing as someone you are not. An imposter may try to pass himself off in his essay as a seriously committed poet, for example. Yet, if the rest of his application makes no reference to writing poetry, working on publications or taking poetry courses, readers may think twice about accepting his word. Consistency helps. Barry Taylor of the Tufts admissions office cites the case of the student who wrote an impassioned essay decrying the evils of apartheid. Yet nothing in the applicant's record showed a particular interest in human rights, in politics or in any current issues for that matter. His views on apartheid, a fashionable issue, seemed to have been pulled off the editorial pages of a newspaper. Susan M. Hart, Associate Dean of Admissions at Hamilton, adds, "Our object is to learn more about *you*. We can read about South Africa in *Newsweek*."

John E. Stafford, a college admissions counselor, tells his clients, "Pick a topic you care about, an issue of significance and familiarity

Before you write about South Africa, march in an antiapartheid parade.

to you." Nothing will flop faster than an impersonal essay full of sweeping generalizations about a big issue that has puzzled scholars or politicians for years. "Avoid warmed-over social studies," warns Douglas Arnold of the Duke admissions staff, "and write instead about a subject that is personal—something important in your life." If you're going to write about South African racial policies, make sure you can demonstrate real knowledge and personal interest. Have you, for example, marched in an antiapartheid parade, written letters to your representatives in Congress, collected names on a petition or at least spoken out about the subject in your history class?

Andy C, applying to Boston University, weakened his chances of getting in by starting a one-and-a-half page essay about the state of planet Earth in this manner:

> In this day and age environmental problems are very important worldwide topics of discussion. These controversial issues have a great effect on all of society. . . . I am very concerned about what is happening to our habitat.

Andy was probably sincere, perhaps even gravely worried about global pollution, but there is nothing personal or persuasive about his concern.

Harry Bauld, a former admissions dean at Brown and Columbia, says that those vague statements that go on and on about the environment, nuclear war or world hunger are called Miss America essays. Like beauty queens, they recite platitudes and offer simpleminded solutions to the stickiest problems. "The world would have peace if only Russia and the United States sat down and had a good, heart-to-heart talk," wrote one "contestant" rejected by Hobart.

In contrast, Peter D, applying to the University of Denver, laid claim to a serious interest in Greek politics at the outset of an essay on elections in Greece:

> Through my mother I am a Greek citizen. She came from Greece and thought it would be a good idea for her children to hold dual citizenship. . . .
>
> Even though I am very Americanized, I still have strong ties to Greece. At home I often speak Greek, I eat Greek food, read Greek magazines and even listen to the news from Athens on shortwave radio. Although I have a lot of American friends, I'm closer to the Greek friends I have at my church. Each summer I go to Greece for about a month to visit my relatives. When I am older, I may go there to live. I don't know yet.
>
> Lately, I have been watching closely the Greek elections and the consequences. . .

Write a Unique Essay—the One That Only You Can Write

Even essays on topics of vital personal interest don't guarantee success, of course. Sometimes you can hardly tell one from the other. They sound almost mass-produced. "We don't expect Pulitzer Prize essays," says Karen Ley, an admissions associate at Lafayette, "just good honest efforts that tell us something about the individual writer."

When he began his essay for the Air Force Academy, Tom M didn't realize the pitfalls of assembly-line writing:

> I would like to attend the Air Force Academy because I want a good college education. I also want to learn to fly, become a military officer and serve my country.

"So do 8000 other applicants," Tom's high school English teacher told him. "What's going to set you apart from every other candidate?" It was fortunate that Tom ran his essay through several drafts. His first effort would certainly have earned him a letter of rejection because it lacked a hook to catch the eye of an admissions official. Much later, after numerous drafts, Tom had a hook:

> "Five. Four. Three. Two. One. Blast off!"
> My friend Eric pushed the button and a red rocket, about as long as my forearm and less than half as wide, whooshed into the sky. It almost disappeared from view before we saw the opening of a small white parachute that would bring it safely back to earth. "Wow-eee," Eric and I shouted as we sprinted toward the landing site as fast as our 11-year-old legs would move. Another successful launch by the founders and only members of the Linden Street Junior Birdman Club!

Tom then recalls that his love affair with flying sprouted during his days as a rocket maniac in sixth grade. Although Tom finally decided not to apply to the Air Force Academy, the magnetism of his new opening paragraph may well have stopped his folder from slipping unnoticed into the rejection pile.

Jim R, an applicant to Duke, responding to the question, "What is it you do that best reflects your personality?" devised a uniquely personal approach. He wrote a list of forty sentences, each beginning with *I*:

> I love music of every kind.
> I have never been rock-climbing, but I intend to go soon.
> I share a room with my kid brother who is a dirt-bike maniac and who often drives me up the wall.

> I hate to sit in front of people who talk in the movies.
> I grow weepy over stories of faithful dogs like Lassie and Buck.
> I could survive very well on a diet of spaghetti and Dr. Pepper.

Thirty-four sentences later, no reader could fail to recognize Jim, the person behind the essay.

When a college asks you to describe your interests, be cautious. Don't let your passion for karate, military history or sailing distract you from the purpose of the essay—to tell the college about yourself. Stay clear of the temptation to write a *World Book* article on black belts, famous battles or boats. Matt S couldn't resist writing about the subject he loved the most. He began (and continued) in this fashion:

> One of my main interests is cartography. Some day I hope to work for the U.S. Coast and Geodetic Survey, the federal agency responsible for making and maintaining maps for the government and the public. Mapmaking is fascinating, especially because maps keep changing. Most people think that the land never changes, but with road construction, dams, floods, earthquakes, storms and fires, many maps made 40 or 50 years ago are now obsolete. One of the most dramatic cartographic changes in the United States has been on Cape Cod, Massachusetts. Every decade the ocean coastline recedes 30 feet and the bay shoreline grows a similar amount. The place where the pilgrims landed in 1620 is now a quarter of a mile offshore.

Few high school students study maps as avidly as Matt. In spite of his unusual passion, however, his essay, which sounds much like a geography textbook, got a chilly reception in a college admissions office.

Focus on a Single Area

Although Matt hid his personality in facts and statistics, he had the good sense to focus his essay on a single topic. Not everyone does. Here, for example, is the opening of Nancy B's essay for Ohio Wesleyan:

> My 4 years in high school have been very rewarding and productive. As well as receiving excellent grades, I have become involved in many of the extracurricular activities offered at the school. Although at times I have been dissatisfied with some of my classes, I am generally enthusiastic about activi-

ties, and this enthusiasm has added a lot of life to the school atmosphere.

In addition to academic achievements, I have developed a strong sense of leadership. This is evident in the positions I have held during the past 4 years as elected representative to the school government, captain of the lacrosse team, cochair of the assemblies committee and editor-in-chief of the yearbook. . . .

Because Nancy had already listed her activities on the application, she squandered a chance to give Ohio Wesleyan more information about herself. She buried a lively personality in an essay that reads like a list of activities. Shirley Levin, an educational consultant from Rockville, Maryland, says, "It's far better to convey a feeling of pride, achievement or accomplishment in a very small area."

Don't repeat in your essay what you've written someplace else on your application.

Elissa G did just that in her Bryn Mawr application. Long a frustrated math student, she focused sharply on her ultimate victory over arithmetic, as this excerpt shows:

. . . I never did get the hang of adding anything with more than one digit. I still have to think twice when multiplying six and eight. Moreover, I am completely reliant on my pencil and paper. The most annoying facet of this whole disability is that I understand and like math. Algebraic theory fascinated me, geometric proofs thrilled me and logarithms were amazing. Yet, I kept messing up tests and problems because I multiplied wrong, or added wrong or subtracted wrong . . . thank heaven for partial credit! Finally, in my sophomore year, I was rewarded for my rudimentary deficiencies. After maintaining a B average in my Trig class for a whole year, I whizzed the Regents, got a 100 and received an A in the course.

Focusing on a single area may be tough when you've done a lot with your life. By targeting one activity, though, you can show how hard you've thrown yourself into it. You can also include specific details about yourself, details that make you sound more like a real person. Consider, for example, this excerpt from Susan F's essay for Brown University:

My most rewarding acting experience was at the Andover Summer Session. I played the ruinous young girl, Mary Tilford, in Lillian Hellman's *The Children's Hour*. The role was very different from those I was accustomed to, like the good-natured nurse, Nellie Forbush, in *South Pacific*. Mary is a sadistic, tantrum-throwing, spoiled child who can also present a most ingenuous exterior. To show her complex personality—the manipulative female, the affectionate grandchild, the nasty friend—was difficult for me. I have a tendency to repress all anger, and when Mary was alone with her peers she was vicious. In one scene I had to slap a girl who is a good friend. To make the slap believable I had to really hit her. This was almost harder than the hysterics or the cloying sweetness, but with practice was finally perfected. To my pleasure, some of the audience did take my portrayal seriously. I had several students stop me in the cafeteria and with horrified expressions exclaim, "You're so mean!" Fiction had been transformed into reality—perhaps the best review.

The Boasting Problem

Susan wanted Brown to know of her triumph on the stage. She was rightfully proud of her accomplishment, yet didn't sound boastful. Since most of us have been taught not to boast, we don't usually puff ourselves up too much. We don't want to appear conceited. Still, Shirley Levin tells college applicants, "Look, if you don't blow your horn, nobody else will." The problem, though, is that self-impressed people rarely impress others. So, if you're good at something, tell the college, of course, but don't shout. A champion with touch of reserve or a sense of humor is always more endearing than a braggart.

Be proud of your achievements, but don't brag.

Mike M is a gifted political cartoonist, justifiably proud of his accomplishments. He injects droll humor into all his drawings. Yet in this passage from his New York University essay, which focuses on his gift, he sounds smug, maybe even arrogant:

> I would like to direct the attention of the admissions committee to my extensive involvement in political cartooning for the past 4 years. The responsibility of producing no less than one satirical drawing per week has necessitated my regular reading of the *New York Times* and other news publications, such as *Time* and *U. S. News and World Report*. As a consequence, I have become well-informed on issues of national affairs and American foreign policy. In the future, I anticipate using my knowledge and artistic talent to raise the social consciousness of the ordinary citizen by pointing out the issues that I feel are of great importance.

Mike was accepted, but surely not for being the sort of person his essay portrays.

Similarly, a high school senior named Eliot M, evidently dazzled by his own musical achievement, didn't realize how immodest he sounded when he told Tufts:

> My extraordinary talent and accomplishments in the field of music are sufficiently noteworthy to warrant my inclusion in the highly selective all-county orchestra.

Although Eliot may deserve respect for his musicianship, he could probably use a lesson in modesty.

Actually, modesty is rather easy to learn. Just say that you consider yourself lucky to have great talent, or after telling how you've struggled to attain success, add that you're still trying to do better. For instance, Suzanne W, another exceptional musician, wrote on her Yale application:

> As a violinist, I have discovered wonderful feelings of accomplishment, surpassed only by the knowledge that it is only the beginning of a lifetime's experience.

Roger D is also blessed with excellence. He loves art and knows a lot about it. In his Columbia essay, he showed how well-informed he is by relating an incident in the art museum:

> As I was standing in front of *St. Francis in Ecstacy,* two college students came over and started discussing the painting because they had to answer questions about its symbolism, composition and use of color for their art history class. Realizing that they weren't getting very far on their own, I decided to help. I pointed out religious symbolism and mentioned Giovanni Bellini's influence on Venetian painting—his use of sensuous colors and perspective. They seemed impressed by what I said, and I don't know which I enjoyed more—talking about the painting or looking at it.

The simple phrase, "I don't know," rescues Roger from sounding vain. More than that, though, he got a kick out of using his knowledge to do a good turn for someone else.

Of course, excessive pride may not be your problem. Like most people, perhaps, you don't have an extraordinary talent. In fact, you may be searching for something in your life that's worth writing about. Don't worry. Everyday life has been the source of many exceptional essays. In your school locker, in your work as a checker at ShopRite, in your close ties to a grandparent, you may find kindling for a good, sharply focused essay. For Tufts, Dave K wrote about delivering newspapers to lonely senior citizens. Every day he became an old woman's link to the world. Kenny D, applying to Michigan, described his fight against boredom as a stock clerk at a supermarket. As he unpacked boxes he became a student of shopping carts, discovering that consumers express themselves by their choice of groceries.

Dangerous Area: Proceed With Caution

The "jock" essay

Although no essay topic is off limits, some contain pitfalls that you should avoid. Admissions personnel, for instance, are rarely impressed by the so-called jock essay, the one that predictably tells the reader what you learned from being first-string left tackle or playing goalie on the field hockey team. Every reasonably successful athlete has learned self-discipline, courage and sportsmanship on the field. If a sport has truly been a crucial part of your life, your essay will have to show how. You'll have to do more than write the story of how you won the race or how losing it helped to build your character, however.

In his college essay, Mario B claimed that he learned the meaning of individuality out on the wrestling mat. The lesson may not be particularly fresh, but Mario's opening paragraph bursts with his gung ho spirit and enthusiasm:

> I am a wrestler. Although wrestling is not as popular a sport as basketball or baseball, it is the most challenging of interscholastic sports because it is always one-on-one. Sometimes in a basketball game, a player will slam-dunk a basket, but he has four teammates on the court with him. In baseball, the pitcher will strike out the side, but he has eight men behind him when a batter hits the ball. In wrestling, though, it's always one-on-one. Nobody else is responsible for your wins or losses. When I win, I feel great, but when I lose I know that I alone have to work harder the next time.

Brian C, a fencer, wrote a more unconventional jock essay for the University of Pennsylvania. As these excerpts show, Brian invites you into his mind during a match:

> "Fencers ready?"
> "Ready, sir."
> "Fence!"
> . . . I must win this bout. I have to be careful; I must find and exploit his weakness without allowing him to ensnare me in his strength. Every fencing bout starts like an argument: In the beginning, one must be patient and find out where one's opponent stands on the issue, before going in for the kill. When I was a child I would always lose arguments. Afterward I would go home and think of things I could have said to win. When I entered high school, I joined Model Congress, an organization patterned on the U.S. Congress.

After 3 years, it has improved my verbal fencing immeasurably and I find that now I rarely lose an argument.

. . . He advances; I retreat, extend, lunge and miss. He moves in for the riposte. Panicking, I make a wild parry; he coolly disengages and I feel his point on my chest.

"Halt!" yells the director. "Touch left. Score is 3–1. Fencers ready?"

I am upset. He's scored three times as many touches on me as I have on him. If the bout continues like this, I will lose! This sport is silly; poking people with metal blades! I could be reading a book now. Reading is a wonderful pastime because every time I read I learn something new. When I read, I empathize with the characters. I feel new feelings and think new thoughts. Every book I read makes me more complete.

As he thrusts and parries, Brian also thinks about skiing, sailing, doing his physics homework and traveling. In fewer than 500 words, Brian's personality and interests unfold. He reveals his intellect and sense of humor, his versatility and writing skill. Because the piece covers so much of Brian, an admissions dean wouldn't err badly by accepting Brian into the college solely on the strength of his essay.

Last summer I went to . . .

At almost any college, Brian's essay would outclass most others, especially those written on such common topics as athletics, working as a camp counselor, a wilderness adventure and travel. Traveling, in fact, is probably the most popular subject chosen for college essays. Applicants seem extraordinarily fond of turning their travels into "significant experience" stories. Travel has virtues galore, but writing about it can be perilous. Colleges take a dim view of essays that are little more than personal narratives of "My Trip to Niagra Falls" or "What I Learned About Myself While Biking the Berkshires." Parke Muth, assistant dean of admissions at the University of Virginia, reports that he sees up to 3000 essays a year on students' travels. "I never knew that travel could be so tedious," says Karen W. Ley, assistant director of admissions at Lafayette, who sometimes reads thirty accounts of summer trips in one night.

> **Travel is probably the most popular subject for college application essays.**

Once in a while, though, someone writes a gem of a travel essay, like this one that David M sent to Berkeley:

My German teacher, Mr. Turner, has decorated his classroom with Lufthansa posters showing scenes of the Black Forest, fairy-tale castles on the Rhine and the mountains of Bavaria. There's also a beautiful sunset in Cologne, with the cathedral silhouetted against the orange sky. They are all hung there to show what we would see if we traveled to Germany, which I did last summer.

> In preparing for my trip I packed my 35 mm camera and a
> dozen rolls of color film. I wanted to be ready to take photos
> of all the picturesque sights we would encounter during our 3-
> week trip. Strangely, I came back to the United States with
> ten rolls of film still in their boxes.

In the rest of his essay, David tells of how his attitude toward photography changed after meeting an elderly Dutchman, Mr. Gillem, in the memorial museum at Dachau, the site of a World War II concentration camp. Gillem, an art historian, talked with David at length about the uses of photography and convinced him that taking snapshots of pretty scenes merely wasted film. Pointing to photos depicting the horrors of the Holocaust, he told David to use his talent to awaken people to the wrongs of the world and to leave the scenery to postcard photographers. David closed with this paragraph:

> I took just forty pictures on my trip, mostly of people I
> met: Dore, a pretty girl in Hamburg, some Swiss students on
> the Rhine, a professor and his wife in Heidelburg and a family
> friend I stayed with in Karlsruhe. Also I bought about a
> hundred postcards and a travel poster for my German teacher.
> Mr. Gillem would be proud.

David's travel piece differs from most others because it focuses on an encounter with just one person. Notice, too, that the trip changed David in only a small way. He now thinks differently about taking photographs. This is a modest change and is far more credible than the grandiose claims made in countless college essays about how a summer trip transformed a student's life.

Maureen McDonnell, a Northwestern University admissions counselor, thinks most applicants who choose to tell about their travels "are not pushing themselves creatively and intellectually." So, unless you pick a fresh approach, store the memories of your trip in a scrapbook. Don't turn your unforgettable summer into a forgettable essay. For example, Tim C, an applicant to the University of Rochester, went traveling to New England and Canada, but his essay went nowhere, as this opening paragraph shows:

Don't turn your unforgettable summer into a forgettable essay.

> An experience that has had a great meaning for me oc-
> curred the summer of my junior year. During that summer I
> spent a week in Maine, a week in Vermont, and a week in
> New Hampshire. I also visited Quebec for a briefer period of
> time. My trip away from home led me to mature and to ob-
> tain a better and broader picture of how other people live.

If Tim had left blank spaces where he wrote Maine, Vermont and New Hampshire, you could fill in Maryland, Virginia and North Carolina or, for that matter, any other state or country on earth.

The result would be the same—failure to convey the uniqueness of the experience.

Harry Bauld has labeled essays that fail to stand out "the noose with which a 17-year-old can hang himself." John H. Henry, assistant admissions director of the University of Vermont, agrees that the "textbook response" to a question works against an applicant. When you're reading hundreds of essays, observes Daniel M. Lundquist, an associate in Penn's admissions office, "they really get repetitive after a while."

Answering the Offbeat Question

Many colleges, hoping to draw out the uniqueness of an applicant's personality, make unusual requests on their applications. Penn asks you to send page 217 of your 300-page autobiography, Stanford wants to know what you'd stow in a time capsule and Dartmouth tells you to write your own question and answer it. Bates asks you to write your own recommendation, and Goucher instructs you to invent something and discuss it.

Such questions aren't meant to catch you. They don't have correct answers. It doesn't matter at Goucher whether you invent a cure for AIDS or a digital belt buckle. Colleges just want to know you better and see if you can think and write. When Swarthmore asks you to travel through time, choose a stopping place and explain your choice, they're not interested in your mastery of history—your transcript contains that information. They'd rather hear why you picked the Jazz Age or the day Mt. Vesuvius exploded.

An offbeat question doesn't obligate you to write an offbeat answer. Just make your answer sound like you. Doug Brooks, a Duke admissions counselor, advises, "If you are naturally creative, write a different, off-the-wall essay." If creativity isn't your strong suit, be sincere. "Everyone has the capacity for sincerity," adds Brooks. You'll never be penalized for a clearly written and thoughtful essay that accurately reflects your beliefs and feelings.

If faced with an oddball question, beware of being too cute in your response. When Stanford asked, "What adjective do you think would be most frequently used to describe you by those who know you best?", one jokester replied, "terse," and didn't write the essay. University officials were not amused. In contrast, they were charmed by Elissa G's answer:

Beware of being too cute. If creativity isn't your strong suit, be sincere.

> It's a nice little word—"intriguing." It carriers that suave nuance of smoky cafes and *Casablanca* or a James Bond

movie. All of which are not exactly appropriate, since I could never imagine myself in a sleek, black evening gown, picking up a tall handsome guy in a wild, Latin nightclub only to have my romance completely spoiled by my father's kidnapping, etc. How boring. I'm not knocking the connotation though. I rather like being a dark and mysterious lady.

Yet "intriguing" is just a bit more than a connotation. It's the ability to interest people and to keep them interested. It's a slightly contagious enthusiasm that interests people—that attracts them to you, your ideas or your activities. That is something I certainly can do. For I can help triple the size of the Debate Team, or try something new with the yearbook or surprise a close friend with an innovative idea . . . and with any luck, I can intrigue you.

In her first paragraph Elissa toys with the meaning of her word, but in the second she reveals its substance. Any admissions official would be "intrigued" by Elissa and want to know more about her.

Answering the Ordinary Question

An oddball essay question may inspire quirky answers but an ordinary question shouldn't tempt you to write an ordinary response. A typical question—this one from Bates—may ask, "What personal or academic experiences were particularly rewarding for you (a project, teacher, piece of writing or research, a particular course of study)?" Although the question suggests that you write about school, you are free to pick any experience whatever. You may be better off, in fact, if you choose

Take the less-traveled route; choose a topic that's distinctly yours.

a unique personal experience. Finding your own topic demonstrates your initiative. You can also bet that most other people will play it safe and write about school. Don't run with the crowd—unless you know that you can beat them. Otherwise, take the less-traveled route. Choose a topic that is distinctly yours. (See Chapter 3 for lots of suggestions.)

Unusual creativity is not essential. You can bring out your best in a sober, sensitive and sincere essay as well. Just don't get caught in the trap of dry, long-winded and empty prose, like the writer who began his self-appraisal this way:

During one's 4 years in secondary school, one's education is centered around a number of different things that hopefully will be helpful in college and in the career one pursues.

Yes, the point may be understandable, but the writing is dull and impersonal. Compare it to a statement like this:

> I wonder if what I was taught in high school will help me
> in college and afterward. If not, I will be very disappointed.

At least you hear a person's voice in those words, and that's what colleges listen for.

College admissions people generally agree that the worst essays are those that summarize the writer's high school career. Nevertheless, students keep pumping out boring recitals of what they did since ninth grade. Nina G. Crowell, an associate admissions director at Yale, thinks she knows why: Competition to get into the "hot" colleges drives high school seniors away from risk-taking. Aiming to please, over half the applicants to selective colleges write safe, dull essays.

Hoping to inspire more potent writing, Holy Cross tells high school seniors "to be open and creative, serious or humorous, since this is your opportunity to convey to the Board those qualities and thoughts which make you distinctive from other applicants." Even though equivalent advice isn't specifically stated on your own applications, you can't go wrong to assume the same guidelines apply, no matter how ordinary the question.

Humor in Your Essay

Although essays that contain gimmicks, like puns, coined words, slang and fractured English, may attract attention among thousands of ordinary essays, your attempt to be clever may poison your application. An ill-timed wisecrack could miss the funny bone of a weary admissions dean. This doesn't mean you should avoid humor. On the contrary: since you have plenty of opportunity to be sober and serious in the rest of the application, in the essay you can give your wit a workout. Readers will relish something playful, satirical or whimsical. Don't overdo it, though. Tread lightly and cautiously with jokes and sarcasm. What you and your friends may think is uproarious in the school lunchroom could fall on its face in the admissions office. Test your humor on an impartial adult before you send it to a college. If you're not usually a funny person, don't try to become one on your application. Bill Cosbys are not made overnight.

Sometimes gentle, self-effacing humor is best. No one at Harvard, for example, objected to Lisa E's tongue-in-cheek account of why she no longer dreamed of becoming an Amazon explorer:

In your essay you can give your wit a workout.

I would not make a very good adventurer for two reasons: motion sickness and ignorance. I am particularly prone to seasickness—an unfortunate circumstance, since the proper way for adventurers to travel is in boats, preferably shipwrecked ones. As for ignorance, I am prone to ignorance in all areas; although in this case I am referring only to my ignorance of jungle survival tactics. I would undoubtedly perish within 24 hours of my arrival in the Amazon by drowning in a bog, treading on a sleeping snake or ingesting a poisonous species of mushroom or grub. Then again, I might be stricken by some dread jungle malady or consumed for brunch by the very tribe of cannibals I had intended to study. Even worse, I might finally arrive in the Amazon only to find myself accosted by vendors of tribal nose rings and "I survived the Amazon" tee shirts.

In writing about a significant experience for Penn, Joel B poked fun at his own ineptness as an outfielder in a childhood baseball game:

The game begins. Joel stolidly assumes his usual position in right field. Anxiety dominates his emotions. He is forced to stand outside on a field on a hot and sticky day, surrounded by clouds of swarming gnats. He fears that a ball may never be hit to him, and the only thing more fearful than that would be for a ball to be hit to him. His pet peeve on the baseball diamond is the "easy" pop fly. Joel wishes that people wouldn't include the word easy every time that phrase is used. He could be back in school demonstrating his academic prowess. Yes, school is a place where little Joel could shine! No one could hold a candle to his mastery of multiplication tables. Not to mention spelling. *There* is a field in which he could compete with the best of them.

In Sabrina E's essay for the University of Chicago you also find humor, but humor with a bite:

Before I arrived in my present high school, I attended school in Ireland. There are many differences between American and Irish education, not the least of which is the priority placed on actual teaching. Though in America scholarship comes first, in Ireland more time is spent trying to keep us on the paths of virtue than in steering us toward the paths of wisdom. Indeed, it seemed that a veritable legion of nuns was employed solely to safeguard our morals.

Whenever one of our regular teachers was absent, we were treated to one of Sister Assumpta's lectures. This latter-day saint was, by her own account, in direct communication with God. Apparently, each night as she prepared for bed, she would fall into a trance and converse with Him. This meant that whatever she told us came directly from the horse's mouth, although we were more inclined to believe that it came from the opposite end of the same animal.

Knowing that her irreverence might disqualify her at some colleges, Sabrina sent the essay anyway. She took a gamble, but for her it was worth it, since she wouldn't have wanted to attend a college where her humor wasn't appreciated.

Whether the application questions are cute, common or challenging, all colleges have the same basic reason for asking applicants for one or more pieces of writing. As the Columbia application puts it, "Write an essay that gives the Committee on Admissions a sense of you as an individual." Colleges are "making every attempt to admit *people*, not simply academic machines," according to Therese P. Overton of the Wesleyan admissions staff.

As you begin to think about how you'll present yourself as a person to the college of your choice, keep asking two key questions: What's unique about me? and What do I want my reader to think of me? In your answers you're sure to find the seed of an essay that will work.

Reading Your Essay

Like customers, readers are always right. Maybe you won't like what they think about your essay. Maybe they'll misunderstand your intentions. They're still right. They get what they get—it's that simple.

Even the best writers can't always predict how readers will respond to their work. That's why you should plan to show your application essay to an unbiased reader or two before you submit it to a college. Ask your readers to tell you their impressions of the writer. If their impressions coincide with what you've intended, you're likely to have written a successful essay.

In the pages that follow you'll be privy to thoughts and reactions of a college admissions officer recorded alongside the text of four essays. Then, you'll see the final evaluation of each candidate's work.

Joyce B

Fairly dull opening. Hope it gets better. Essay has three parts: many interests, simple life and new things. One topic, in depth, would probably be better.

"exposed"? Did she live the life-styles or just observe them?
"early age"? 3? 4? 10? I wonder what she means. What could she have learned at age 3?

If someone were to ask me to describe myself, I would have to say that I am a person of many interests. I enjoy a simple life, yet I am not afraid to try new things.

I have been fortunate enough to become exposed to a variety of life-styles at a very early age. During my travels to Europe I was able to visit Germany, Italy and Switzerland. There, I learned about different cultures and how other people live. Watching and meeting people is one of the many things that I enjoy.

No more travels? Now she's into dancing. How often does she dance? A major pastime?

Ah! She likes to join groups. That's good. I wonder if she speaks Italian.

Good transition. But she's switched her focus again!

Not another topic! Athletics. Well, we can use her on the gymnastics team.

Not much new here. Pretty trite. An example could make this sound more honest.

Oh, no, she's switched again.

OK, she's ambitious and hardworking, but it's hard to tell without more details.

Why were the courses special? Good grades?
She seems diligent. I bet her teachers and counselors say she's a plugger.

She's been busy, all right. How much time could she have given to these jobs? I better check her list of work experience.

What values?

Upbeat ending. But "youth faces tomorrow" isn't too interesting.

Since the age of 4, I have been dancing with "Dance Capri," a countywide Italian-American folk-dancing group. My involvement in this organization has introduced me to people who are interested in some of the same things I am. We enjoy learning about our Italian heritage and pride ourselves in keeping up the folk-dancing tradition.

Along with dancing, traveling and meeting new people, I enjoy skiing and gymnastics. I usually ski in Vermont during my vacations, but last year I had the opportunity to ski in Quebec, Canada, for a week. I have always been on gymnastics teams, during the school year and the summer, and although I never won any special honors, I enjoy competitive gymnastics meets, especially the balance beam. For me, competing with a team has taught me what working for one common cause and reaching one common goal are like.

One of the most relaxing hobbies I enjoy is cooking. When time permits, I bake and I prepare special meals for my family. I learned how to cook through various cooking courses that I took when I was younger. In high school, I could only fit one food preparation class into my program.

Along with this class, I enjoyed a variety of other courses in high school. However, the ones I liked the most were jewelry, Italian and history. I believe, though, that I made the most out of every course I took in high school.

Out of school, I invest a good deal of time in various part-time jobs. My work experience includes cashier and hostess work in an Italian restaurant, and my present job, which is working as a Gal Friday in an insurance office. I also baby-sit when I have the time.

High school was and still is a time of growing and maturing for me. Although working hard and getting good grades has always been my first priority, I also established and set many of the values that guide my life today. I can confidently say that in my senior year of high school I am ready to meet the challenges of college. I am ready to move on, and I see a bright future ahead of me.

Note to admissions committee:

Joyce B's essay suggests an active, but fragmented life. Joyce skids breezily from topic to topic, suggesting just casual involvement in many areas. Yes, she's well-rounded, but so are most of our applicants. I can't find anything to distinguish her from others. After reading her essay, I dont know her very well.

Her writing is essentially correct, but it's boring. Not one of her paragraphs is developed beyond presenting some general facts about herself. Too much of her essay reiterates information already stated in her application. Moreover, Joyce fails to deliver what she promises in her opening passage. Where, for one, is her "simple life"? I recommend "rejection" unless there's evidence in her file that contradicts my impression.

Chandra B

Hmm, a common topic—the struggle of writing an essay.

Well, this is different: The struggle has been worth it. She's learned about herself. I wonder what she's learned.

Perceptive. A good idea! We can't know ourselves completely, can we?

Hmm, a sensitive mother, but c'mon, no mother talks like that. She sounds like a psychology text. Good point, though, and the dialogue adds life.

Vague paragraph. A bit ponderous. I wonder what she's driving at.

Now I see! She's been struggling for an identity. And it hasn't been easy. Her mother was right.

Struggle to communicate? That's splendid! Chandra's a deep thinker.

This is the fourth essay I'm writing, and it won't be any easier than any of the first three. You see, it isn't that I enjoy writing these essays, but with each one I have found out a little bit more about myself, and that is important to me. The purpose of each essay, of course, is to show that I have a sense of who I am, but there is always more to be found at the bottom of the well called "me." I wouldn't be fooling you or anyone if I said I know absolutely, totally everything there is to know about me.

My mother said to me this evening, as she finished reading my third essay, "You know what theme I find recurring in each of these, Chandra? A sense of struggle, of some sort of tension within you. And that, I think, is what drives you. It is helping you in your maturation. Perhaps it needs resolving, but at the same time you know it is there, and you are dealing with it."

I think that for everyone sooner or later there is a time of inner tension and struggle—a time when one asks, "Who am I? What do I mean to myself?" It is those who face this struggle and deal with it rather than deny it, who eventually succeed in being who they want to be. One must learn to make choices about what one wants to stand for, to do with one's life, and at the same time one must learn to change oneself in order to achieve this.

My first essay dealt with a struggle in choosing between a German heritage and a Jewish one. My choice, however, was neither one nor the other, but a compromise to accept both as being part of me, to reconcile rather than to deny. My second essay dealt with a choice I may still have to make, namely between choosing marine biology or genetics as a career. This is a choice I may never have to make, for I may discover something I want to do more than either of them. I have not limited myself to only these two choices. Yet even now, I think I would decide upon marine biology, not because I find it more interesting, for I find them both equally so, but because I enjoy it more; I have more fun with it. My third essay dealt with a struggle I will always face, namely my need to communicate. I feel the need to know about others, and to have others learn about me. This is my way of sharing myself and partaking in others. My struggle is a

She seems high-strung, a little tense. Is that why she's lonely? I wonder what her teachers say.

Ah, she's come back to the struggle again. Conclusion recalls her opening. Nice way to unify the piece.

She's convinced me. I believe she'll win her struggle. Strong, upbeat ending.

fight against misunderstanding and loneliness. When we communicate, whether between people or nations, we understand each other. When we communicate, we bridge the gap of loneliness.

There will always be struggles within me, dilemmas I will face. I am determined to resolve these tensions. With each choice, I choose who I am, who I will become. Most importantly, though, it is I who makes these choices, not someone else. That is what self-determination is all about.

Note to admissions committee:

Chandra B finds life is a serious undertaking. Her writing has conviction. She's not going to play her way through college or engage in foolishness. Her thoughtful—nay, philosophical—ideas attest to her maturity. She probably drives herself hard, maybe compulsively. She seems genuinely bound on a quest to find an identity.

Will she study hard in college? You bet, and will probably get As. Will she contribute to the college? Intellectually, yes, and maybe in other ways, too. Let's accept her and several more passionate thinkers like her. I hope that her teacher and counselor recommendations confirm my impression that Chandra is a rare find.

Angela C

Starts off like another "jock" essay—but very graceful. An appealing opening.

Oh, she's not a jock, after all. Smooth shift from kindergarten to ninth grade.

Well, she's a student and an athlete.

A rich paragraph! Shows Angela's loyalty to friends. Her perseverance, too. And the fun she's had.

As far back as I can remember, I have excelled at sports. I was always the first in my kindergarten class to reach the swings during recess and the first to climb to the top of the rope during gym. However, while most 6-year-old girl athletes tend to develop into "school-yard jocks," I seemed to lack that aggressive, competitive nature. I was much more content reading my book than keeping up with the boys. By the time I entered high school, I was clearly defined as a "student," not a "jock."

When I tried out for the field hockey team in ninth grade, it was merely because a good friend of mine begged me to do it with her. The idea of spending 3 hours every day running around a field didn't particularly appeal to me, but for a friend I'd do anything. After 2 weeks, my friend quit. Quitting has always been anathema to me, but in this case it never entered my mind anyway. I was having fun. Those 3 hours of practice were the best part

And she has other interests, too.

She's well-organized. That shows in her essay.

Good transition. This is moving right along. Angela is a serious hockey player.

She's obviously committed to the sport. Good, detailed writing.

She's a hard driver, too.

Interesting! She took on a challenge and won, and she's proud of her achievement. A good point.

Effective conclusion. She's summarizing her career and showing how she's changed. Good writing.

How successful she's been! And modest, too.

What determination! I think she'll make it. She's unstoppable.

of my day. I loved being outside, and being physically active. Most importantly, I loved being with my teammates. Between studying and practicing the piano, I'd spend so much time alone that my time on the field became a welcome and necessary break in my day. Also, coming home at six o'clock every evening helped me to budget my time, since I knew I only had a few hours in which to complete my assignments.

It wasn't until my sophomore year that field hockey became more important to me than just a social activity. It was still terrific fun since I loved getting to know the juniors and seniors on the team whom otherwise I would never have met. Some of them are still my closest friends. However, playing on the varsity squad was a very different experience from playing on the freshman team. I found myself missing holidays and giving up weekends to play hockey. The team now required a serious dedication and commitment, which I was willing to make since I enjoyed it so much. As my commitment became more serious, so did my attitude toward field hockey. I realized that I couldn't accept being a mediocre player.

Mediocre is one of the most negative words I know. I knew in my sophomore year that, as the new player on the varsity team, I was also an average player. Traveling to Holland with my field hockey team revealed to me again my inadequacies when I saw the skill of some of the Europeans. Since then, by attending camps and clinics and playing in summer leagues, I've really worked hard to become a good player. I always want to be good—if not the best—at everything to which I set my mind. To be a good student comes naturally to me, but for me to be a good field hockey player requires work.

I remember when I first started playing field hockey. I thought that to be an all-county player and captain of the varsity was to be the best. Well, I *am* an all-county player and I *am* the captain of the team but one thing I am certainly not, is the best. Whenever I achieve one of my many goals, it always seems as if a new one appears ahead of me. Now that I'm a good high school player, I'm ready to start at the bottom again and work to become a good college player.

Note to admissions committee:

Angela C clearly demonstrates self-confidence and an upbeat personality. She's good at everything, and she enjoys all she does. Her essay indicates that she's loyal, well-organized, determined, committed to success, industrious and fun-loving. Yet, she doesn't bowl you over with her attributes. Instead, she casually tosses them into the story of her growth as a field hockey player. In spite of all her virtues, she neither brags nor sounds like a Boy Scout. She's an all-round scholar-athlete.

Angela can write! There's not an ill-chosen word or awkward phrase in the piece. Could she have received help? Look for confirmation of writing talent in her grades and references.

My recommendation: If she's really as good as she sounds, offer her the dean's house and a Ferrari!

Eric H

A catchy opening.

Oh, another essay on divorce.

"subsistence materials" Ugh! Does he mean toothpaste, underwear, a week's supply of socks?"

"abode," "commences" Too fancy.

Mother sounds like an ogre, probably the villain in the story.

"asinine" Good word. Eric sounds bitter.

Ah, a good line. Sardonic humor.

I don't get the point of all this. Does he mean that his life is a treadmill? Why doesn't he say so?

Ah, good. There's a bright side to the story.

Well, Dad's no hero either.

Shows maturity and responsibility, I guess.

It is Friday afternoon, a time I can so vividly remember enjoying. School would let out, and no matter how much homework I had, I could always relax Friday and Saturday. Unfortunately, T.G.I.F. has evolved into O.G.I.F. (Oh @#$%, it's Friday!).

Joint custody: an American revolution. Friday is the transition day, the day that a week's worth of subsistence materials have to be transported from one parent's abode to the other's. My room at Dad's has to be cleaned, my clothes washed and pressed and other essentials placed in order. Then my odyssey commences. Somehow, I have to get all of my belongings from one end of town to the other.

Usually, Mom picks me up. She tries to be tolerant but at times loses her cool. "I'm only going to do this once. If you forget anything, that's your tough luck." I try to explain that I can't fit everything I own into her Toyota. Sometimes she forgets that I didn't ask for this asinine way of life. In any event, four trips to the car later, we leave home and head for home.

By the time I'm really settled, another week has passed. O.S.I.F.!, and I find myself out of breath exactly where I started. In the span of 2 weeks I have accomplished nothing except total aggravation. I can't even blink for fear that another Friday will come.

Like anything else, joint custody has its bright side. When my parents were divorced, Dad had a big decision to make: pack up and forget his little brats or remain for the duration. Even though he's never been nominated for any Best Daddy awards, he hasn't regretted his decision to stay.

The entire ordeal has brought us a world closer. When we were quite suddenly hurled into an unamiable apartment without Mom, we shared a common interest: survival. Neither of us knew how to break an egg, sew a hem or clean a toilet bowl.

He refused to learn these things, so I had to. Today, 6 years later, I cook all the meals, do all the shopping and make most of the household decisions in place of my father. He basically grants me a generous expense account

Forty dollars? Only forty dollars? That's hard to swallow!

Puzzling. Didn't he grow close to his father? Something's missing here.

Well, good. He can make jokes, despite his misery.

Who suggested?

Well-stated.

Cute ending.

of forty dollars on Friday night, and it is up to me to see that food is purchased for the week. This burden has done wonders for my character. Many of my friends fear life at college, but not I. If I can tolerate life with my father, campus life will undoubtedly be a breeze.

Another advantage to joint custody is variety. Just when I get sick of the accumulated dishes, dirty laundry and ravenous cockroaches that are a way of life at my Dad's, I can run to Mom's for a week. Come the next Friday, you can be sure that I'll be so fed up with my mother's vexatious organization and fetish for punctuality that I'll welcome cockroaches with open arms. I think that's what is meant by escapism.

It has been suggested that I stop writing essays complaining about joint custody and simply leave half of my stuff at either house. It seems logical. Maybe that's the problem; it makes sense. I don't think divorce and custody were destined by the Almighty to make sense. I suppose I just have some psychological aversion to leaving 50 percent of my life unattended for a week.

All in all, I suppose joint custody isn't so bad. I'm never bored, and I'm always on my toes. Oh @#$%, I've got to run. It's Friday!

Note to admissions committee:

Eric H certainly has courage! He took a personal gamble by writing about an obviously painful subject. It's not that he's looking for sympathy, but rather he chose to vent his anger about being shuttled between his parents each week. He has a right to be bitter, but I question his judgment in using the application essay as a place to blow off steam.

The essay is meant to be humorous, and it is—to a point. The humor is a thin disguise, though, for someone who laughs to hide his tears. My guess is that Eric's anguish makes him hard to like, but I'd like to know what his counselor and teachers think.

He's not a bad writer, although he seems to flaunt his vocabulary—not always successfully—perhaps thinking that college people will be impressed. His work lacks polish, but I think that in time it will improve.

His essay works neither for nor against his candidacy. My recommendation will be based on the other information in his application and file.

3 WHAT TO WRITE ABOUT

ssay question 6 on part 3 of the Brown University application reads:

> In reading and evaluating your application we hope to gain as complete a picture of you as is possible, but our knowledge of you is necessarily limited to the information provided us. Why not, then, use this opportunity to tell us about anything you think we should know?

Why not, indeed! As a Brown hopeful, you probably wouldn't decline the invitation to write an essay. Before you started, however, you'd probably consider more than one essay idea before settling on the one you actually use. Some writers seem to find inspired topics all around them. Others think long and deeply before writing a word. Still others arrive at their topics only after committing words to paper. To prime their creative pumps, they just start writing. Ideas start to flow, and suddenly they discover what they want to write about. (If you're one of those people who often suffers from a shortage of writing ideas, turn to the end of this chapter for a few thoughts on how to tap into a good source of material, namely, your own mind.)

To find a topic for yourself, use whatever method suits you, but stay ever mindful of the intent of your essay—to project personal qualities not readily apparent in other places.

You may think of the essay as a burden, but colleges regard it as an opportunity for you to put the finishing touch on your application, as your last chance to amplify or add information about your background, experience, talent, skills, character, personal philosophy and zest for life.

How do you do all that in an essay of 250 to 500 words? The Sarah Lawrence application recognizes the challenge and simply advises applicants to "be true to the person you have already become, and tell us about that person."

The Topics

Colleges have devised innumerable topics. Some applications offer a choice, and others tell you to write whatever you please—as though to test your inventiveness. Still others lay out specific guidelines for an essay, partly to see whether you can follow directions. Several colleges suggest topics but also offer you a chance to make up one of your own.

Although application essay questions differ in detail from one college to the next, most of them fall loosely into five groups, each with opportunities to project yourself onto paper, but each with perils to watch out for: (1) Why go to college, and why here? (2) Who are you? (3) Would you tell us a story about yourself? (4) What is important to you? and (5) What would you like to tell us about yourself?

Responses to these questions frequently overlap. If, for instance, you were to write on *a significant personal experience*—one of the most popular topics—you'd probably tell a story. The experience you choose would also reveal who you are, and your explanation of its significance would identify some of your personal values.

In the sample questions and topics listed in this chapter, you may not find the exact question your college asks but you'll probably recognize one that comes close.

Why go to college? Why here?

From questions about your plans for the future, colleges hope to discern your route for the next 4 years. What will the college experience mean to you? Will you study, or will you party? Have you thought about why you're going to college at all? Expecting a look at your educational map, colleges often make inquiries such as these:

- *Why do you want to go to college?*
- *Why do you want to go to this college, in particular?*
- *What are your career objectives, and how will college help you achieve them?*
- *How will this college help you fulfill your goals and aspirations?*
- *What will your presence add to this college?*

No one answer to such questions is preferable to another. If you aim to be a physicist for IBM, that's fine. Yet no college seeks to fill its classrooms with only one type of student. In the main, colleges try to keep their enrollments balanced. It's not a weakness, therefore, to admit that you don't know how you want to spend the rest of your life. College is for exploring. In fact, liberal arts students frequently come to campuses with receptive and open minds. More than likely, they'll rummage through many of the offerings on which a college has built its reputation.

As you explain your intentions to a college, consider these essay-writing hints:

DO

- Answer the question being asked, not the one you'd like to answer.
- Before writing a word, scrutinize the college's offerings. If you expect to major in, say, ecology, be sure the college has an environmental studies program.
- Think hard about what *you* hope to get out of college, avoiding clichés, such as "I want an education," "I want to get a good, well-paying job" and "I want to be a success in my chosen field."
- Try to figure out why this college appeals to you. Did the college representatives make it sound exciting? Did you visit the campus and get good vibes? Is there a particular program that has attracted your interest?
- Focus on educational or personal reasons for going to college, not on social, economic or family reasons.

DON'T

- Don't use flattery. All colleges already know how good they are.
- Don't stress that you love the college's location, size or appearance. By applying there, you have implied that those characteristics are acceptable to you.
- Don't tell a college that it's your "safe" school.
- Don't write that you're going to college because you don't know what else to do.

Finally, don't take any of these precautions as the last word in application essay writing. Use them at your discretion. Don't ignore them, though, unless you have a sound reason for doing so. Jim D, for example, came right out and told Bowdoin he wanted to go there precisely because of its location. "Like Thoreau," Jim wrote, "I feel most alive near wild streams and forests."

ANSWERS THAT WORKED

Marian T's afterschool work in a fabric shop inspired her love of fashion and developed her flair for design. "In college," Marian wrote, "I plan to major in fine arts."

David B studied four languages in high school. Because of his bent toward languages and foreign cultures, he wants a career in international affairs as a businessman or diplomat, but he said, "A stint in the Peace Corps will come first."

Lisa C loves to read. "I can't imagine a career more suited to me than librarian in a school or a public library," she wrote.

Wendy W has wide and wandering interests. Last year it was dance, this year it is Greenpeace. Wendy thinks of college as a place for "accumulating more interests, for meeting people, for working hard and, ultimately, for finding a niche in life to fill."

Andy S has always taken the hardest courses. He doesn't know why, except that doing well in tough courses has made him feel good. "I hope to continue feeling good in college," he quipped.

Deena R admires one of her high school English teachers. Since he's told her wonderful stories of Williams College, she'd like to go there, too. "I plan to major in English," she wrote, "and find out if Mr. Stern's stories are true."

Karen S's "most joyful and gratifying high school experience" has been working with mentally retarded children. In college she'll major in special education.

Mark D lost his father and a brother last year. Yet he has retained his essential optimism. He wrote that "there is still a promise in life for me. There are so many things that I have not yet experienced, but inevitably must." That's why he wants to go to college.

Don Z has met many people through playing guitar at festivals and nightspots. He thrives on people whose style of living differs from his. Don asked, "What better place than a giant university is there for finding a variety of people?"

Becky B is thinking of a career in acting. She expects a college education to help her become a more complete person. "My wish," she wrote, "is not only to be a good actor but also a good person, and my belief is that they might be the same thing."

Who are you?

Colleges have heard what others think of you—teachers, counselors, interviewers. With self-assessment questions, they hope to learn what you think of yourself. Do you know who you are? Are you aware of how others react to you? Would you like to change in some way? Self-knowledge is often thought to be a prerequisite for understanding the world, and an essay that demonstrates that you know yourself will give your application a big boost. To check the depth of your insight, colleges ask questions like these:

- *What is important to you?*
- *How would you describe yourself as a human being?*
- *How might a freshman roommate describe you?*
- *Write your own recommendation to college.*
- *If you could strengthen one aspect of yourself, what would it be? Why?*
- *What quality do you like best in yourself? What quality do you like least?*
- *Imagine yourself as a book or other object. How would people react to you?*
- *What makes you different from other people?*

In your response, readers hope to find clues to your personality. Unless you present yourself as a bizarre monster, they won't necessarily care whether you are soft-spoken or loud, a realist or a dreamer, a liberal or a rock-hard conservative. They'll give you short shrift, however, if they think you are a fake. Above all, then, in writing, "who are you?" essays, be truthful with yourself—as truthful as you've ever been before.

Telling the truth doesn't mean you must bare your soul.

Telling the truth doesn't mean you must bare your soul and disclose your deepest secrets. Colleges don't need to know about your sex life, psychiatric treatment or drug and drinking problems. On the other hand, you needn't portray yourself as a saint. Students have written successful essays about their cynicism, frustration, greed and favorite vices. In the end, let good taste govern your choice of material. If you have doubts, switch topics. Jenny G wrote an essay about a family drug problem, thought the better of it afterward, and wrote another, highlighting her good judgment.

DO

- Answer the question that is asked.
- Be as honest as you can. Search for qualities you really have, not those you wish for.
- Emphasize specific, observable qualities that show your distinctive personality. Imagine that your reader will someday have to pick you out in a crowd.

- Illustrate your qualities with specific examples. Use telling anecdotes to support your opinions of yourself.
- Ask people who know you well whether they agree with your self-analysis.

DON'T

- Don't be evasive. Stand up for what you think about yourself.
- Don't be too cute or coy. Sincerity is preferable.
- Don't choose a characteristic merely to impress the college.
- Don't write everything you know about yourself. Focus on one or two of your outstanding qualities.
- Don't write an essay fit for *True Confessions*.

Remember that you can violate every rule and still write a compelling essay. Just be aware of the perils.

ANSWERS THAT WORKED

Suzannah R thinks of herself as a dynamo in danger of burning out by age 20. She can't control her energy level. She's impatient and often intolerant of others' laid-back attitudes. She added, "As I have grown older, I feel I am learning to accept other people's shortcomings."

David V said, "The most important fact to know about me is that I am a black person in a white society." David considers himself an outsider and expects to continue feeling alienated as long as racial prejudice exists.

Ellen E contrasted her goofing off early in high school ("personal problems and just plain stupidity") with her productive junior and senior years. In effect, she was reborn during the summer between tenth and eleventh grades.

Allison R has fought shyness all her life. She recounted three moments in her life when shyness defeated her. In contrast, she told of three recent incidents that have helped to raise her self-esteem.

Steve M sees himself as a latter-day Clarence Darrow, always standing in defense of the little guy, often taking the minority point of view in class just to generate a little controversy. If others consider him obnoxious, he claimed, "it's a small price to pay for a life full of heated debates and discussions."

John K sees himself as a character in a movie. When he's alone he pretends he's Richard Dreyfuss, playing the role of a yuppie bachelor. He even hums background film music when he's driving and jogging.

Brendan B is a gourmet cook. He loves to eat. "You are what you eat," he believes, so he defined himself by the food he enjoys most. From meat and potatoes, for example, he has gained a strong will. From French sauces, he has derived a subtle sense of humor.

Nicole W is a perfectionist. From schoolwork to keeping her room in order, she cannot allow herself to do anything shabbily or incompletely. She is worried about "getting a slob for a college roommate."

Dena P, a gymnast since age 8, works like a demon to be number one. Ever striving for perfection, she wrote, "I know now that when it comes to making commitments, I can be ready to make them."

Doug M is an adopted Korean orphan. He sees himself as a child of two cultures. Although a double identity causes confusion in others, he feels "more fortunate and richer" than his American classmates.

Jennifer B loves computers. Everything about computers comes so easily and naturally to her that she said, "I sometimes think that I must have been born in an Atari factory. Instead of brains, maybe I have memory boards and microcircuitry inside my head."

Would you tell us a story about yourself?

Telling stories is a most natural thing to do. When you come home from school you tell what happened that day. You tell friends what Donna said to Fred and how Kathy felt afterward.

The story you write for a college application isn't expected to be like a superbly crafted tale by Poe or O'Henry, just an autobiographical account of an experience. It should tell about something that happened and what it meant to you. A good story both entertains and informs the reader. A story written for a college does even more. It suggests your values, clarifies your attitudes and, better yet, breathes life into your personality.

Although storytelling possibilities are limitless, application questions usually direct you to identify and discuss a noteworthy time in your life:

- *Write about a significant experience or event in your life and what it meant to you.*
- *Write an original essay about a humorous personal experience.*
- *What is it that you have done that best reflects your personality?*
- *Describe a challenging situation and how you responded.*
- *Comment on an experience that helped you discern or define a value you hold.*
- *What is the most difficult thing you've ever done?*
- *Write about a group endeavor in which you participated, and describe your contribution.*

In response to any of these topics, you can write a story about last night or pick an event from the time you wore diapers. The experience can have been instantaneous or long-lived, a once-in-a-lifetime occasion or a daily occurrence. It can have taken place in a schoolroom, a ballroom, a mountaintop—anywhere, in fact, including inside your head.

Almost anything you do from the moment you wake up has possibilities.

An event need not have been earthshaking to inspire a story. Almost everything you do from the moment you wake up holds possibilities. If you haven't noticed how life is crammed with moments of drama, cast off those blurry lenses and start to look for the hidden realities behind the daily face of things: In a disagreement with your brother, in an encounter with a former girlfriend or in a teacher's criticism you may find the ingredients for an insightful, dramatic essay. Simply by making a list of ten things that happened yesterday and another ten things that occurred last week, you may trigger more than one essay idea.

If you want to write about the time you made headlines, that's great, but most people lead ordinary lives. To take a common experience and interpret as only you can is a perfectly acceptable way to think about the task before you.

DO

- Answer the question that is asked.
- Choose an experience you remember well. Details will make or break your story.
- Pick an experience you can dramatize. Let the reader hear people speaking and see people acting!
- Focus on a specific incident or event.
- Make yourself the central character in the story.

DON'T

- Don't think that a commonplace event can't be turned into an uncommonly good story.

- Don't choose a complicated event unless you can explain it briefly. Fill in background, but focus on what happened.
- Don't lie. If you must fabricate material for effect, be sure it sounds like truth.
- Don't ramble. Rambling stories are boring.
- Don't explain your point with a lecture on what the reader is supposed to notice. Let the story make its own point.

ANSWERS THAT WORKED

Ted B collects things: matchbox cars, license plates, matchbook covers and rocks. From his hobby he has learned about design, geography, advertising and geology—and interior decorating, too, for after 5 years of collecting, he literally wallpapered the foyer of his house with matchbook covers.

Pete S was riding in a car with his brother. At a stoplight a pretty girl in a neighboring car smiled at him. Pete looked away. Afterward, he berated himself and resolved to become more outgoing and more responsive to others.

Colin V is Catholic. Last year on May 6 his Jewish godson was born. As a result, Colin's eyes have been opened to the world of Jewish customs. "I look at everything differently now," Colin wrote.

Jenny B's hard-of-hearing grandfather lives with the family. Whenever Jenny tries to help the old man, he rebuffs her. A blowup occurred after Jenny knocked too loudly on his door to summon him to the phone. The incident has caused her to reflect at length on the needs of the aged.

Mary G, from a middle-class family, works in a slum area soup kitchen with her church group. She'll never be a social reformer, but the work, she claims, has made her "more sensitive to the needs of the poor and homeless."

Roy O's summer at a lake with his father building a cabin gave him time to think about how lucky he was to have been born in the United States into a fairly well-to-do family. "I'll never take the blessings of life for granted again," he wrote.

Liz H and her twin sister Mary have rarely been apart. Lately, Liz has found it necessary to seek her own identity and has taken up running as a way to get away. Her hours of solitude on the road have helped to strengthen the bonds with her sister.

Sandy M says, "Sunday is always spent gathering the scattered fragments of my life." It's the day she uses to catch up on schoolwork, gain some perspective on her social life, make peace with her parents and look in the mirror for a long time trying to figure out who she is.

Lauren S has always been plagued by insecurity. An offhand remark by an art teacher (Hey, you're good!") has helped her to build confidence and work that much harder in her courses. She's beginning to see signs of how good she really is.

Lisa R's parents were divorced. The complex legal negotiations that accompanied the split, while painful to her, so fascinated Lisa that she plans to become a lawyer.

Robert S thinks that he has been ostracized at his school because of his ragged appearance. Instead of wearing a jacket and tie to an honor society interview, he showed up in his jeans. The incident heightened his awareness that people are judged by superficialities, not by their character.

What is important to you?

Would you rather hear a Bach cantata or a Grateful Dead album? Would you prefer to go bowling or spend an afternoon in an art museum? Do you like fast foods or nouvelle cuisine? To a great extent, your preferences define you. Hoping for a glimpse of your taste and your biases, many colleges ask you to write a "choice" essay. Rather than give you a menu of choices, however, they tell you to come up with one of your own—your favorite quotation, an influential person in your life, a significant book you've read:

- *What is your favorite quotation? Explain your choice.*
- *What have you read that has had special significance for you? Explain.*
- *Identify a person who has had a significant influence on you, and describe that influence.*
- *Tell us about a personal, local, national or international issue of particular concern to you.*
- *What is your favorite noun? What does it mean to you?*

- *If you could invent anything, what would you create? Discuss.*
- *If you could affect the outcome of human history by changing a particular event, what event would you choose? How would you change it, and why?*
- *If you could spend an evening with any prominent person—living, deceased or fictional—whom would you choose, and why?*

What you choose when responding to such questions is important. But the rationale for your choice is even more important and should make up the heart of your essay.

The key to a writing a forceful response is that your choice has some direct, personal bearing on your life. A quotation from Shakespeare may sound impressive, but if you pick it only for effect, you'd be better off with a lyric from David Byrne or a maxim of your grandmother's. Before you select an important world issue like terrorism or overpopulation, be sure you've been personally touched by it. Instead of condemning war, tell what you've done to support peace. If you write on a book, don't limit yourself to school reading. What you've read on your own tells far more about you than any class assignment.

If you are wavering between two equally good choices, tip your scales toward less popular subjects. Conversations with Columbus, Shakespeare and Lincoln have already been written. So have numerous essays about cures for cancer and AIDS. Many students have already written about altering human history by eliminating war, preventing the birth of Hitler and scrubbing the flight of the space shuttle *Challenger*. They also have expressed concerns about affirmative action, nuclear power, abortion, capital punishment, poor people and women's rights. Countless others have been influenced by a grandparent, a sibling with a handicap, a teacher or a virtuous public figure.

Nevertheless, the last word on all these subjects hasn't yet been written. Although admissions staffers may frown on still more essays about peace or pollution, they'll welcome any essay that's genuine, insightful and interesting.

DO

- Answer the question that is asked.
- Choose a subject that you care about.
- Let your head and heart be your source of material.
- Think of at least three very good personal reasons for your choice.
- Try out more than one answer. Submit the one that you like best.

DON'T

- Don't choose a topic merely to look good.
- Don't be self-conscious about your choice. Just tell the truth.
- Don't choose a subject that requires research. Let your experience guide you.

ANSWERS THAT WORKED

Lisa D, born in South Africa, came to the United States at age 11. Her antiapartheid essay recalls her black nurse, who was forbidden to enter the park where Lisa and her friends played hopscotch and tag.

Amy B thinks that Hawkeye from television's "M*A*S*H" would make an ideal dinner companion. She admires Hawkeye's humor, his understanding and his impatience with hypocrisy. As for his sexist attitudes, wrote Amy, "On this issue the Hawk and I don't see eye to eye."

Barbara B has been fascinated with space flight ever since second grade when the elementary school librarian introduced her to a science fiction book, *Matthew Looney, the Boy from the Moon*. In college Barbara expects to major in physics or astronomy.

Luke J chose the word *family* as his favorite noun. To explain, he wrote a moving portrait of a close-knit family. Five times in the last 10 years the family has moved. Luke's father works overseas for months at a time, Yet, Luke derives stability from his family, despite its fragmented life.

Robert B refuted the old adage, "You can't compare apples and oranges," by writing a tongue-in-cheek comparison of the two fruits. As a result, he wonders about the validity of other pieces of wisdom. He plans to research next "You can't tell a book by its cover" and "Absence makes the heart grow fonder."

Carl G, who has a deaf kid brother, wrote about *Dancing without Music—Deafness in America*, a book that persuaded him and his parents to introduce young Danny to other deaf people as a way to help the boy find an identity as a hearing-impaired person.

Gary K wrote about Steven, his mentally retarded brother. All his life, Gary has been Steven's fun committee, psychiatrist-at-home and teacher. Gary wept recently after he found Steven eating pineapple from a can. It had taken Gary 6 weeks to teach Steven how to use a can opener.

Jordana S said that her favorite cartoon character, Linus from "Peanuts," has qualities that she envies: stability, self-confidence and grace under pressure. As for his security blanket, "Linus carries it to show that he's secure enough not to worry what others think about his carrying it."

Joanna L named Miss B, her elementary school gym teacher, as a significant person in her life. Miss B so intimidated Joanna that "even today the smell of a gymnasium and the sight of orange mats stimulate feelings of terror and dread."

What would you like to tell us about yourself?

erhaps the toughest writing assignment is the one without a suggested topic:

- *We would welcome any comments you care to make about yourself.*
- *The essay is an important part of your application. It will help admissions officers gain a more complete picture of you. Use the essay to tell about yourself.*
- *If there is anything else you would like to tell us about you, please explain on an additional sheet.*
- *Please use this page to give us any information you think would be helpful to us as we consider your application.*
- *The purpose of this application is to help us learn about you.*
- *Is there additional information we should know that will help us to make an informed decision?*
- *To better understand you, what else should we know?*

Without restrictions, you may literally send in anything. Starting from scratch, you can cook up a totally new piece of writing. Or you may submit a poem, a story or a paper you've written for school or for yourself. Applicants who have written for publications often send samples of their writing. If you include a previously written piece, don't just pull it from your files and throw it in the envelope. Carefully explain on a new cover page what it is and why you chose it.

Avoid submitting a reheated essay, one you've written for another application.

A word of caution: Avoid submitting a reheated essay, one you've written for another application. A college that asks an open-ended question won't appreciate an essay entitled, "My Most Significant

Academic Experience" or "I'd like to spend an evening with . . . ." Naturally, you can use bits and pieces from your other college essays, but rework your material, disguise it, change its focus—do all you can to keep the college from suspecting that you're sending in a secondhand sample of your work. In a pinch, you may of course need to send the same essay to two or more colleges. On the other hand, your essay may be so good you feel compelled to use it again. In either case, courteously tell the second or third college what you have done and why. Your decency will be appreciated.

DO

- Pick something important—something that matters to you.
- Consider explaining anything unusual that has influenced your school or home life.
- Use a style of writing that sounds like you.
- Write the sort of piece (e.g., essay, poem, internal monologue) you've written successfully in the past.

DON'T

- Don't turn down the college's invitation to write more about yourself.
- Don't put on airs to try to impress the college. Be yourself.
- Don't repeat what you've written elsewhere on your application.
- Don't try to use a form or style of writing for the first time unless you have a record of successful writing experiments.
- Don't write the essay (or any other part of your application) the night before it's due.

ANSWERS THAT WORKED

Bonnie W asserted that writing the college essay helped her sort out her feelings about herself. She has finally accepted the fact that she is a nonconformist. "I used to run with the 'in' crowd," she wrote, "but now I don't give a damn. I can breathe."

Lillian S, a student of karate, wrote about how it feels to break a board with her bare hand. Writing about karate, she said, has heightened her concentration as she trains to earn a black belt.

Dave E reflected on violence in America. His thoughts had been triggered by a triple murder that had occurred a few weeks earlier in a neighboring town.

Kevin B wrote a funny piece on being a New Yorker. On a recent trip to Massachusetts with the school band, his overnight host expected him to come equipped with a switchblade and chains. The folks in the Bay State seemed disappointed by his "normal" behavior and appearance.

Jenny J wrote a collection of fables, each concluding with a moral or maxim to illustrate a strongly held conviction. One story ended, "Be satisfied with who you are." Another, "Don't turn your back on anyone in pursuit of power."

Adam B wrote a piece detailing the first time he baked walnut tarts. Like an expectant father, he paced the kitchen floor, waiting for the oven bell to sound. At the gong, his whole family rushed in for a taste. The verdict? "Well, that night I retired with a grin on my face," wrote Adam.

Ray G, a high school basketball player wrote a tongue-in-cheek analysis of his statistics. Last season he batted .300. He also got 600 on his math SAT. "Does that mean my math is twice as good as my hitting?" Ray asked. "I doubt that my math teacher would say so," he added.

Jodi F wrote about a family trip to Europe. Her parents were on the verge of separation, but during the tour of Italy, France and Spain her mother and father made peace. How odd, thought Jodi, "to save my home by leaving it."

Barry G wrote of waking in the middle of a hot summer night and going to the roof of his apartment building for some air. Peering at the lights below, he experienced a self-revelation. As an intelligent person, he realized that if he set his mind to it, he could do almost anything he wanted to with his life. Thinking of possibilities, he stayed on the roof until dawn.

Pamela M reviewed her dancing career since age 4 and concluded by stating, "Dancing has allowed me to express myself from within and to be, feel and love who I am."

Thinking of Ideas to Write About

If you're one of those blessed writers who explode with ideas for every assignment, read no further. You don't need this section. If, however, you routinely come back empty-handed from topic searches, try some of these popular do-it-yourself techniques for spawning ideas.

1. If your essay due date is weeks or months away, start a journal today! Innumerable college essays have begun life as journal entries. From now on, record whatever catches your eye or tickles your brain. Anything! Since no one else will see what you write, literally everything is OK. Some of what you write may be silly and pointless, but not if you force yourself to tell the truth and only the truth.

   Frankly, your honest images and thoughts may lead to a dead end, but journal keepers often run into rich veins of ideas in their daily entries. After a few days, a journal begins to be a source book of information on you. When you need a topic for your college essay, you'll have a personal reference book at your fingertips. In its pages you may discover the stuff to write the essay of your life.

2. Try free-writing. That is, write nonstop for 10 to 15 minutes a day, paying no heed to grammar, spelling or punctuation. Concentrate on telling the truth about whatever is on your mind that day. You'll be amazed at how rapidly ideas flow when you write un-self-consciously and without preplanning. After free-writing you won't have a polished essay, or even a first draft, but you might have bagged one or two surprisingly fertile ideas.

3. Focus your free-writing. Once you have done some free-writing, reread what you've written. Circle any idea or phrase you like or that holds promise for an essay topic. Take one of the ideas that feels right, and free-write on that one. When you focus your free-writing, you accumulate possibilities on a topic. The human mind spits out thoughts so speedily that most of them vanish before they reach consciousness. In free-writing, though, you can preserve thoughts before they get away. Try focused free-writing again and again, until you've arrived at a satisfactory essay topic.

4. Like pulling out a stopper, making a list often starts the flow of ideas. A list of items, quickly jotted down, may bring to mind just the topic you're looking for. Writing down lists of influential people in your life or books you've read acts like a simple word-

association exercise. As your mind makes connections, one name calls up memories of the next and the next. Anything and anyone can go on your list. At first, don't be particular. Later you can start to be discriminating as you narrow the choices for a possible essay topic.

5. On a very long sheet of paper—perhaps several pieces of attached computer paper—create a time line of your life. Write down every event you can think of, whether you think it's important or not. Ask people whom you've known for a long time to suggest additional items for your time line. A perusal of the finished work may suggest lifelong themes, key events and personal interests that can be turned into essay topics.

6. Talk to anyone who'll listen—a teacher or coach, a boss or a soulmate also in search of a topic. When you least expect it, one of you might just blurt out the very idea you've been looking for. Besides, when you solve a problem with someone else, you often get a bonus called synergism—the combined power of two heads working together, which usually exceeds the total power of two heads working separately.

4 COMPOSING YOUR ESSAY

You probably won't get out of high school without writing some sort of essay on *Macbeth,* or if not *Macbeth,* then on the Great Depression or dissecting a frog. By this time in your life, in fact, you've probably written enough essays to fill a large book. When writing those essays, perhaps you sat down, spilled your thoughts onto the page and handed in your paper. Maybe you wrote a rough draft and went back later to reorganize and rephrase your ideas. Possibly, you thought out ahead of time what you wanted to say and prepared a list of ideas or an outline. Maybe you used a combination of methods, varying them from time to time according to the importance of the essay.

Everyone who writes uses a process of some kind. Some processes seem to work better than others. The variations are endless, however,

The process you use to write is as personal and unique as your fingerprints.

and the actual process you use is as personal and unique as your fingerprints. Since it is personal, let me step out of my role as writing instructor for a moment and describe the process I used to write this chapter so far.

Before I typed a word, I had a general idea of what I wanted to say: namely, that anyone facing an essay question on a college application has already had plenty of writing experience and that the same process a person used to write essays in school can be used to write an essay for college. Furthermore, I wanted to assure the reader that no single process is better than any other, as long as it works. With those thoughts floating around in my head, I started to write, hoping that one idea would lead smoothly into the next. I also hoped that extraneous ideas wouldn't lead me away from what I had in mind, something that frequently happens when I write.

Fairly rapidly for me, because I'm usually a very slow writer, I typed the first two paragraphs. Then I reread them. Luckily, they seemed to stick to the topic and they more or less expressed my thoughts. I wasn't altogether happy with my opening sentence, however, which originally read, "By this time in your life you must have written a ream of essays." I thought that some of my readers wouldn't know the word *ream*, so I changed the sentence to one that would surely evoke an image of a lot of pages: "By this time in your life you must have written enough essays to fill a large book."

A moment later, however, I decided that even that sentence wasn't right for an opening. I needed an idea that hit closer to my readers' experience. So I inserted two new sentences, turning my original first sentence into the third. Still later, I added the phrase "in fact" to that sentence, intending to bind the thoughts in the first three sentences more closely to each other.

As you see, I like to write a few paragraphs as quickly as I can, then return to them before going on. I don't always do that, however. Sometimes I write more, sometimes less, before doubling back to rewrite and edit. Other writers work differently, and so, no doubt, do you.

If you compare my original opening paragraphs, reproduced below, with the printed version at the state of this chapter, you'll discover several more changes, each intended to make the writing clearer and more interesting. All the while, I kept thinking of you, my reader. I figured that if you are going to spend time reading my words, the least I could do is make the time worth your while. I also wanted to make you feel compelled to read on. If the phone rang while you were reading, I was hoping you'd be annoyed at the interruption.

> By this time in your life you must have written a ream of essays. In fourth grade, remember writing about "My Trip to Disney World?" More recently, perhaps, you wrote about irony in *Macbeth* or Chinese immigration to the United States. When you wrote those essays, you probably used a technique that seemed right for you. Perhaps you just sat down, spilled your thoughts onto the page, went back later and reorganized and rephrased your ideas over and over. You may have thought out what you wanted to say ahead of time and prepared some sort of list or outline of your ideas to guide you as you wrote. You may have used a combination of methods.
>
> Everyone who writes anything uses a process of some kind. Some processes seem to work better than others for certain writers. The variations are endless, however, and the actual process you use is personal and as unique to you as your fingerprints. Since it is so personal, let me step down from my post as giver of information about essay writing for a moment and describe the process I used to write this chapter so far.

Thinking About the Reader

You and I have made a kind of agreement. Simply by reading these words, you have agreed to let me enter your life. Thanks. My end of the bargain is harder. I have to keep writing until I'm finished, but you can stop reading at any time.

I don't want you to stop, however. So as I write, I try everything I can to hold your interest, to keep your mind and eyes fastened to these words. That's a tough assignment. Since you're a stranger to me, I don't know what you'll understand or what will grab you. I have to keep guessing. Even if my guess is wrong, I can't stop, can't go back and try again. If you shut this book right now, I'll never know it. No physical force in the universe is strong enough to keep one small muscle in your head from shifting your eyes away from this page. Only the compelling power of my words, along with some lucky guesswork, can do it.

As a writer of a college essay, you face a challenge similar to mine, except that you can be pretty sure your reader will stick with

Writing an essay is a lot like giving a gift to a friend. You try to please.

you to the last word. Because you have a reasonable guarantee of an audience doesn't make the job of writing any easier, however. You're still obliged to give the readers something they want to read. Writing the essay is a lot like giving a gift to a friend. You think about what your friend would like, you try to please, you choose carefully and you present the gift as stylishly as you can. If all goes well, you get a reward for your effort.

But first, it's work.

Warming up

Once you know the questions on your application, you're likely to start thinking about what to write. As you reach into your background to search for a subject, don't lose heart if you come up empty-handed at first. You may need a warming-up period to help you find a subject and prime you for the vigorous mental work ahead. In fact, the ultimate quality of your essay may depend in part on your warm-ups.

For most students, the high school years rush by like a raging river. It's hard to stop and step back a moment to reflect on your life, on how far you've come and where you'd like to go. Now, on the verge of applying to college, is the right time for you to try.

Start with a personal inventory. The key word is *personal*—for your eyes only. Think of who you are and how you got that way. You might begin, for example, simply by making a list of adjectives that describe what you like about yourself. Then make another list of what you dislike. Don't worry if the second list is longer than the first—most people are pretty hard on themselves. Study these lists for patterns, inconsistencies and unusual combinations. For instance, Gina S, whose list appears below, considers herself both "generous to others" and "self-centered." Is Gina contradicting herself? Is she being untruthful? Does she change from time to time? Since the list is personal, no one but Gina needs to know.

Gina's Personal Inventory

What I like about myself	*What I dislike*
loyal to my friends	my nose
idealistic	short temper
trusting	uncomfortable with strangers
determined to succeed	need a lot of sleep
mysterious	living in the past
ambitious	impulsive
competitive	lack of athletic talent
generous to others	can't carry a tune
insightful about myself	gluttonish
sensitive to others' feelings	envious of friends (sometimes)
good listener	overconsiderate of others (sometimes)
good memory	hate math
energetic	often late for appointments
flirtatious	self-centered
	stubborn
	basically shy
	indecisive

Once you complete a list, rank the qualities in order of importance. Which quality would you be most reluctant to give up? Which would you give up first? Which are you proudest of? Which would you most like to change? Answers to such questions define you and begin to draw out your uniqueness, for no one else is likely to respond precisely as you do.

Most items on your own personal inventory will differ from Gina's. Yet, it shouldn't surprise you to find some similarities. Although no item may immediately strike you as the focus of a distinctive essay, a few imaginative connections could lead you directly to a suitable subject. Notice how Gina might have developed several possible subjects from her inventory:

Gina claims to be "competitive," but she also "lacks athletic talent." Her competitive nature, therefore, may emerge in the classroom instead of the gym. Perhaps she competes to win awards as the best reader, writer or mathematician. She may compete for recognition on the job or at home. Regardless of the place, Gina's need to excel could be the focus of her essay.

Gina says she's a glutton, presumably for food. Since a college doesn't necessarily need to know that, Gina could turn gluttony into a metaphor and focus her essay on being a glutton for success. Perhaps she derives satisfaction from being a successful student, friend or member of a particular group.

Gina also says she's "impulsive." In a way, her "short temper" confirms that she occasionally rushes into things. On the other hand, she might point out that her impulsiveness gives her an urge to help anyone in need. Her essay might focus on an incident that demonstrates her unusual generosity. A brief discussion about becoming a social worker some day would add a fitting conclusion to her essay.

Ultimately, Gina found her subject in an incident that would not have occurred unless she truly had a "good memory." This excerpt from her essay tells what happened:

> I had just come from the elephant house at the zoo when I spotted Bucky, my old swimming counselor at Camp Merriwood. It was 6 years since I saw him last. I remembered him only in a Princeton tee shirt and a swimsuit and never imagined that he even owned long pants and a parka, but I recognized his face instantly. I called out his name and introduced myself.
> He looked at me and said, "Oh, I remember you, Gina," but I knew he was just being polite. To him I could have been Jenny, Margie, Eva, Ruthie, Debbie, Abby or any one of the dozens of squealing 10-year-old girls at camp that summer.
> We talked a little while about people and events at camp. No, he didn't really remember the kids on my relay team. Well yes, he only had a faint memory of the swim meet we won against Camp Harding, in which I won two races.
> "What are you up to now?" he asked. When I told him I was looking for a summer job, he said his company sometimes hired high school students in the summer and that I should apply.

Gina landed a summer job in Bucky's firm doing something called "customer relations," a glamorous term for helping to keep the files straight. Gina observed in her essay, though, that she was glad to be working at all. Then she added:

> I got the job as a result of having a good memory. Since then I have become more interested in memory and how it works. I have read some books on the subject and have learned some ways to improve my own memory. In less than a minute I can now memorize ten vocabulary words or the names of ten people I never met before. Elephants are not supposed to forget, which may or may not be true. However, I wonder if remembering Bucky was related to my visit to the elephants in the zoo.

Gina launched her essay with a short anecdote meant to illustrate her good memory. For every quality you list on a personal inventory try also to think of evidence that proves that you are indeed what you claim to be. A single example is all it takes to get an essay underway.

Another place to locate essay subjects is in your answers to a set of questions such as these:

- *What are you good at?*
- *What are you trying to get better at?*
- *What has been your greatest success? Your greatest failure?*
- *What three words would you like engraved on your tombstone?*
- *What is your strongest conviction? Would you die for it?*
- *What would you do with a million dollars?*
- *If the world were to end a year from today, how would you spend your remaining time?*

Thoughtful answers to often whimsical questions may trigger any number of essay possibilities. As you toss ideas back and forth in your head, keep your distance from stock responses—those that will lump you with the crowd. Walk around for a few days letting yourself think about what makes you unique. Tell someone what's on your mind. Keep a notebook in your pocket, because a great thought may hit you at any time. Keep pen and pad by your bed to record a four in the morning inspiration. Do some free-writing. Think hard about what you want your readers to think of you. In short, do something to activate your writing muscles.

Some people call this part of the process "prewriting." You might call it getting yourself "psyched." Whatever the name, it's the time you spend messing with possibilities and tuning up to write. It may even include finding a quiet, uncluttered place to work, gathering together a pen, paper, a typewriter or word processor and a dictionary. It involves laying aside many hours of time for solitary, unhurried work.

Prewriting may include finding a quiet place for hours of solitary, unhurried work.

Warm-up time should also include a search for the point, or focus, of your essay. Identifying a subject isn't enough. Now you must focus on what you'll say about the subject. The sharper your focus, the better. You can't expect to write everything in a 300- to 500-word essay.

Maybe the surest way to narrow your subject is to begin writing. If your essay seems dull and disappointing after a couple of paragraphs, you're probably being too vague, too impersonal or both. Keep going, for you may discover the point of your essay at any time. Be prepared, however, to recognize that you may occasionally write yourself into a dead end. Not every subject works. If you find yourself blocked on all sides, you have no choice but to grit your teeth, turn to another topic and start over.

If you end up dry, even after several attempts, you might try this twenty-question technique for unlocking ideas. Write your subject at the top of a page. Then ask twenty questions about the subject, leaving plenty of space for writing answers. Linda W, for example, knew she wanted to write an essay on dancing, but she didn't know what to say about it. At first she wrote, "During the last 8 years dancing has provided me with great satisfaction." Because every devoted ballerina feels exactly the same way, however, Linda realized that the idea is basically boring. So Linda started asking and answering questions like these:

> What kind of dancing do I like the most?
> When did I first fall in love with dancing?
> Why doesn't everybody dance?
> What would my life be like without dancing?
> Who has been important to me in my dancing? Why?
> If I could not dance, what art form would I use to express myself?
> What am I giving up or sacrificing by devoting so much time to dance?
> How good a dancer am I? How can I find out?

The first questions were easy. When the questions grew hard, both to ask and to answer, Linda had begun to dig deeply into her topic. In figuring out answers, she finally discovered an original point to make in her essay:

> To me, dancing is the most dynamic and personal of the arts. Pictures and sculptures are displayed in museums. Poems and stories are hidden in books. To make music you play someone else's notes on an instrument made by another person. But dancing, ah, dancing, is like life itself.

Where Linda crossed over from prewriting to actually composing her first draft is hard to say, nor is it really necessary. What counts is that she found a topic, narrowed its focus and made a point.

Writing the Essay

By the time some writers begin to compose their essays they more or less know that they'll reach their destination using the famous five-paragraph essay formula. Other writers will start more tentatively, knowing their general direction but not finding the specific route until they get there.

Neither method is better than the other, for much depends on the subject matter and intent of the writer. The first method follows a simple, clear-cut formula, which may not win a prize for originality but can help to turn a muddle of ideas into a model of clarity. It has a beginning, a middle and an end.

The formula is the Chevy of organizational plans—not too exciting, but very practical. You may have already used it in school for answering a test question, analyzing a poem or reporting lab work. You can call on it anytime you need to set ideas in order. Its greatest virtue is clarity. Each part has its place and purpose.

```
The formula

Introduction
                        { Point 1
Body                    { Point 2
                        { Point 3
Conclusion
```

In reality, however, writers rarely follow *the formula*. In fact, you may never see a formula essay in print. Yet a majority of college essays, even those that take circuitous paths between the beginning and end, adhere to some sort of three-step organization. In the *introduction,* writers tell readers what they plan to tell. In the *body* they tell. In the *conclusion* they tell what they told. Since all writers differ, however, you find endless variations within each step, as you're about to see.

Introductions: hooking the reader

Use the introduction to let readers know what they're in for. Don't, however, make a formal announcement of your plan: "This essay is about poverty in the South Bronx." Just state your point. The reader will recognize the topic soon enough, even without a separate statement of your intention. Maria G, for example, began her essay this way: "Working one weekend a month in Mother Theresa's Soup Kitchen in the Bronx with the St. Augustine Teen Club has changed my life." This opening promises the reader an account of Maria's weekends in the slums and what the experience has meant to her. It also sets the essay's boundaries. Maria can't include everything about dismal conditions in the South Bronx. Instead, she'll concentrate on her own experience there, and no more.

The best essays usually begin with something catchy, something to lure the reader into the piece. Basically, it's a hook—a phrase,

The best essays begin with a "hook" to catch the reader's interest.

sentence or idea that will nab readers' interest so completely that they'll keep on reading almost in spite of themselves. Once you've hooked your readers, you can lead them anywhere.

Hooks must be very sharp, very clean. They must surprise, inform or tickle the reader in an instant. A dull hook just won't do. Here are a few samples of each:

DULL HOOK My difficulty in dealing with my feelings probably all started when my parents' marriage started breaking up.

SHARPER HOOK The first thing I remember is my parents arguing in the next room while I was trying to sleep.

The sharper hook is vivid. It creates a compelling image of a child in the dark, attempting to block out the sounds of his parents' shouting. It also provokes curiosity. The reader wants to know more.

DULL HOOK The book, *The Divine Comedy*, is a serious work of literature, written by Dante several centuries ago.

SHARPER HOOK Dante's *Divine Comedy*, despite its title, is not a funny book.

The second hook contains a small surprise for the reader. No one knowing Dante's work, about the author's travels through Hell, would think of it as humorous. Yet, a student coming to the title for the first time might expect to be amused. The mistake is worth a chuckle—but only if you're familiar with the book.

DULL HOOK Among my various extracurricular commitments, music has been the most enduring.

SHARPER HOOK I have tried to immerse myself in music.

In the sharper hook, the terse declaration of the writer's commitment to music makes the point quickly. As the reader, you know instantly that music is the topic. Moreover, the repetition of the "m" sound has a certain appeal.

Your opening should be appropriate to your topic and tone.

Naturally, your essay's opening ought to be appropriate to your topic and tone. A serious discussion of Mother Theresa's Soup Kitchen probably shouldn't begin with an irreverent story about a nun. Beware also of any introduction that's too cute or precious. Be thoughtful and clever, yes; obnoxious, no. If you quickly want to lure your reader into your essay, consider any of these five common methods:

1. Start with an incident, real or invented, that leads the reader gracefully to the point of your essay.

"How about 'John Henry' in A?"

The banjo player kicks off the tune with a solid lead and is joined by the other field pickers in a couple of seconds. Having sung the first verse and chorus, I strum along on the guitar and let my mind wander. How incongruous for me, a product of upper-middle-class suburbia, to be standing in the middle of a grassy field picking bluegrass and old-timey music until dawn.

—**Steve M**

2. State a provocative idea in an ordinary way or an ordinary idea in a provocative way. Either will spark the reader's interest.

If you've never been 6 feet 7 inches tall like me, you probably don't know what it's like up here. Everybody is a comedian when they meet you. They call you "Beanpole," or ask, "How's the weather up there?" or tell you to "Watch out for low-flying planes!" Not only that, they expect you to play basketball, have bumps on your head from doorways and know things that shorties don't.

—**Andy S**

3. Use a quotation—not necessarily a famous one. Shakespeare's or your grandmother's will do, as long as it relates to the topic of your essay.

True ease in writing comes from art, not chance,
as those move easiest who have learn'd to dance.

—Alexander Pope,
An Essay on Criticism

It took me 8 years to understand Pope's message. I know now that he should have said, "True ease in dance comes from wonderful, frustrating, exciting, tedious, time-consuming, strenuous and sweaty work, not chance." That may not sound as good, but it's as true.

—**Lisa B**

4. Knock down a commonly held assumption or define a word in a new and surprising way.

No doubt you've heard that Latin is a dead language. Wrong! Latin is alive and well and living inside my head, thanks to a wonderful teacher who emphasized the culture, not the conjugations, in the language.

—**Alicia G**

5. Ask an interesting question or two, which you will answer in your essay.

"Tell me, in God's name, why you, Terry D, want to become an English teacher!"

"Because . . . because I want to teach," I stammered. I bent my head, hoping my answers would satisfy him and defuse the unbearable tension that stalked about me.

"Come, Terry, that's not the reason; there's more to it than what you've said. Now why do you want to teach? Is it the kids? The classroom? Power? What force within yourself causes you to associate English and teaching?"

—Teresa D

In any collection of good essays you'd no doubt find other equally worthy techniques for writing a compelling opening. Even a direct statement that introduces your topic may be appropriate. Whatever your opening, it must fit your writing style and personality. Work hard at getting it right, but at the same time, not too hard. An opening that seems forced may irk your reader, and one that comprises, say, more than a quarter of your essay is probably too long.

If you can't find a suitable opening when you begin to write your essay, don't put off writing the rest. As you write the body of the essay, a pleasing idea may hit you. Some writers begin by writing three paragraphs, fully expecting to throw away the first two. They need at least two paragraphs to hit their stride and to rid their minds of extraneous ideas. By the time they've reached paragraph three, they've figured out the point of their essays. Only then do they turn to writing a hook. You might try a similar technique. If your throwaway paragraphs contain ideas you can't do without, make room for them later in your essay.

The body: putting the pieces together

To build a house you must start on the ground. On your foundation you construct a frame, then add walls, a roof, a TV antenna—and you're done! The builder must follow this order or the house will crumble.

Order is important to the writer, too. What should come first? Second? Third? In most writing the best order is the clearest order, the arrangement your reader can follow with the least effort.

Just as a highway map shows several routes from one town to another, there is no single way to get from the beginning of a piece of writing to the end. The route you take depends on the purpose of the trip. The order of ideas in the body of your essay will vary according to what you want to do to your reader. Whether you want to shock, sadden, inspire, inform or entertain the reader, each purpose will have its own best order. In storytelling, the events are often placed in the sequence in which they occur. To explain a childhood memory or define who you are, to stand up for gay rights or describe a poignant moment—each may take some other particular arrangement. No one plan is superior to another, provided you have a valid reason for using it.

The plan that fails is the aimless one, the one in which ideas are arranged solely on the basis of the order in which they popped into your head. To guard against aimlessness, rank your ideas in order of importance either before you start or while you're writing drafts. Although your first idea may turn out to be your best, you probably should save it for later in your essay. Giving it away at the start is self-defeating. To hold your reader's interest, it's better to work toward your best point, not away from it. If you have, say, three main points to make, save the strongest for last. Launch your essay with your second best, and tuck your least favorite between the other two.

To hold the reader's interest, work toward your best point, not away from it.

In a typical college essay, a body consisting of three sections will be just about right. Why *three*? Mainly because three is a number that works. When you can make three statements about a subject, you probably know what you're talking about. One is too simple and two is still pretty shallow but three is thoughtful. Psychologically, three creates a sense of wholeness, like the beginning, middle and end of a story. Each point doesn't necessarily receive equal treatment. You might manage one point with a single paragraph, but the others may get more. Each point has to be distinctive: Your third point mustn't be a rerun of the first or second.

It shouldn't be difficult to break the main point of most essays into at least three secondary points, regardless of their topic or form. A narrative essay, for example, naturally breaks into a beginning, middle and end. A process is likely to have at least three steps, some of which may be broken into substeps. In an essay of comparison and contrast, you ought to be able to find at least three similarities and differences to write about. A similar division into thirds applies to essays of cause and effect, definition and description and certainly to essays of argumentation.

Turn back to the sample essays in Chapter 2. Each of the successful pieces follows the three-part pattern. In rough outline, they look like this:

> **Chandra's essay** (page 27)
> Subject: The struggles within me
>   Point 1: What do I stand for?
>   Point 2: What should I do with my life?
>   Point 3: How can I communicate with others?
>
> **Angela's essay** (page 28)
> Subject: My field hockey career
>   Point 1: Starting out in ninth grade—a social activity
>   Point 2: In tenth and eleventh grade—fun and dedication
>   Point 3: Becoming a champion—a serious commitment

Eric's essay (page 30)
Subject: Joint custody
    Point 1: Description of my weekly ordeal
    Point 2: My relationship with mother and father
    Point 3: How joint custody has changed me

Only Joyce's essay (page 25) defies analysis into three sections. In fact, the piece fails for the very reason that Joyce tried to make more than half a dozen points. Each point remains undeveloped, and in the end the essay is little more than a list of Joyce's interests and activities.

Transitions and paragraphs: taking readers by the hand

Readers need to be led. As you write, think of readers as tourists and your essay as a trip they take from one place to another. You are their guide, their travel agent.

After you've told them where they're going (the introduction), keep reminding them (in the body of the essay) where they're headed. In long essays readers need more reminders than in short ones. To keep readers well-informed, you don't have to repeat what you've written, but rather plant key ideas, slightly rephrased, as milestones along the way. (The sentence you just read contains just such a marker. The phrase *"To keep a reader well-informed"* prompts you to keep in mind the topic being discussed—that is, helping readers find their way.) Watch out for detours, for you may lose your readers if you step too far outside the path you laid out at the start. (The sentence you just read is a detour. Yes, it's related to the topic but it steers the discussion away from guiding readers through an essay.)

Help readers along, too, by choosing words that set up relationships between one idea and the next. This can be done with such words as *this*, which ties the sentence you are now reading, for example, to the previous one. The English language supplies many words and phrases for tying sentences and ideas together, among them

also	on the other hand	still
too	consequently	another
further	therefore	finally
in addition	although	in the first place
similarly	moreover	regardless
as a result	nevertheless	on the contrary
however	now	better still
for instance	this	yet

Each time you link one sentence to another with a transitional word or phrase, you help to clear a path for readers through your writing. Without such help, or when every sentence stands unconnected to the next, readers may end up hopelessly lost, like travelers going down roads without signposts or markers.

Links between sentences lend a hand to writers, too. They help them stick to the topic. Ideas that don't connect with others around them probably should be moved or thrown out.

The inventor of the paragraph also figured out a simple way to mark the path through a piece of writing. The paragraph indentation is a signal to readers to get ready for a change in thought or idea, somewhat like the directional blinker telling other drivers that you're about to turn.

Yet, not every new paragraph signals a drastic change. The writer may simply want to move the essay ahead one step at a time, and paragraphs illuminate each step.

Some paragraphs spring directly from those that came before. Like infants, they can't stand alone. The paragraph before this one, for example, is linked to the previous one by the connecting word *yet*. The connection has cued you to get ready for a contrasting thought, but it also reminded you that the two paragraphs are related.

Abrupt starts are best from time to time. Suddenness will surprise and keep readers alert. Connecting words will dilute the impact of the surprise. Be wary of a string of abrupt starts, however, because too many quick shifts may annoy more than surprise.

Paragraphs let your readers skip rapidly through your work, particularly when each first or last sentence summarizes the rest of the paragraph. Readers may then focus on paragraph openings and closings and skip what's in between. Readers in a hurry will appreciate that, but you can force readers to linger a while by varying the location of the most important idea in each paragraph.

Consider your readers absent-minded wanderers. Remind them often where they are.

Whether your readers skim the paragraphs or slog doggedly through every word, they need to find sentences now and then that, like landmarks, help them to know where they are. Such guiding sentences differ from others because they define the paragraph's main topic; hence the name *topic sentence*.

Most, but not all, paragraphs contain topic sentences. The topic of some paragraphs is so obvious that to state it would be redundant. Then, too, groups of paragraphs can be so closely knit that one topic sentence states the most important idea for all of them.

No rule governs every possible use of a topic sentence. A sense of what readers need in order to understand your meaning must guide you. Consider your readers absent-minded wanderers. Since they tend to lose their way, remind them often about where they are. Let the topic sentences lead. If in doubt, grasp their hands too firmly rather than too loosely. Follow the principle that if there is any way to misunderstand or misinterpret your words, readers will most certainly find it.

The conclusion: giving a farewell gift

When you reach the end of your essay, you can lift your pen off the page and be done with it. Better still, you can present your reader with a little something to remember you by, a *gift*—an idea to think about, a line to chuckle over, a memorable phrase or quotation. Whatever you give, the farewell gift must fit the content, style and mood of your essay. A tacked-on ending will puzzle, not delight, your readers.

Some writers think that endings are more important than beginnings. After all, by the time readers arrive at the conclusion, the introduction may have already begun to fade from memory. A stylish ending, though, will stick with them and influence their feelings about your essay and, of course, about its writer. Therefore, choose a farewell gift thoughtfully. Be particular. Send your readers off feeling good or laughing, weeping, angry, thoughtful or thankful, but above all, glad that they stayed with your essay to the end.

Send your readers off feeling glad that they stayed with you to the end.

A conclusion that's too pat or common will leave readers with the impression that you were too cheap to give the best gift you could, or that you chose your gift in haste. Stay away especially from bargain-basement gifts like these:

> The challenges I faced will help me in college and in the future. (from an essay on a significant experience)

> Then I woke up and saw that it was all a dream. (from an essay about talking with a famous person in history)

> I'd recommend this book to anyone who likes good psychological or murder stories. (from an essay about *Crime and Punishment*, an influential book in the writer's life)

> In conclusion, if I can be half as successful as my aunt, I will have fulfilled myself as an individual. (from an influential person essay)

Such trite endings suggest that the writers couldn't think of anything original to say or that they just wanted to get their essays over with. Either way, a stale conclusion can spoil a good essay.

Readers will appreciate almost any gift you give them, provided you've put some thought into your choice. When writing the ending, let your instinct guide you. You've read enough stories and plays and have heard enough songs to know what endings sound like, what lends a sense of completeness to a creative piece of work. For example, when you tell readers how an unresolved issue was settled, or when you speculate on what might occur in the future, readers sense that an ending is at hand.

Even commonly used endings can be turned into stylish gifts, as these samples show.

1. Have some fun with your ending. A reader may remember your sense of humor long after forgetting other details about you.

   SUBJECT **Elizabeth H,** an active member of many groups, treasures the hours she has for herself.

   GIFT Thoreau's remark, "I love to be alone," might well be my senior quote. In spite of the incessant plea of the telephone company to "reach out and touch someone," there are some of us who would prefer to remain untouched. I am one of them.

   SUBJECT **Debbie B's** lifelong competition with her sister Michelle ended when Michelle left for college.

   GIFT . . . I stepped right into my sister's shoes (figuratively, not literally—because Michelle has a size five compared to my seven and a half). I think that my brain would become seriously warped if my feet were that squished.

2. End with an apt quotation, drawn either from the essay itself or from elsewhere.

   SUBJECT **Craig S** had to find safe shelter during a wilderness adventure.

   GIFT At that point I knew by instinct, "This is the place."

   SUBJECT **Frank F** had a part-time job in a hotel kitchen when a terrible fire broke out.

   GIFT To this day, whenever I smell food garbage, I hear the words, "Fire!Fire!Fire!" and the clang of fire bells.

3. Finish with a clear restatement of your essay's main point, using new words. Add a short tag line, perhaps.

   SUBJECT **Carol B** tells how she changed between ninth and eleventh grades.

   GIFT The main difference in me is that now I like myself. I could be friends with someone like me.

   SUBJECT **Ian B** learned about himself while reading Moss Hart's autobiography, *Act One.*

GIFT There are no limits to the human spirit, no obstacles large enough to impede the attainment of a dream, provided that one's resolve and determination are equal to all the discouraging effects of failure. Further, there is no sin in initial failure. That's what I keep telling myself.

4. Bring the reader up to date or project him into the future.

SUBJECT **Ellen G** tells of an old woman she met while working as a volunteer in a nursing home:

GIFT I still visit Mrs. Thurnauer. Some weeks she is more vibrant than others. Even on her bad days I see her intelligence and courage. And even if on a certain day her hair is not combed back as smoothly as when I first met her, she still reminds me that growing old is not always a desperate process, in which all pride and hope are lost.

SUBJECT **Jonathan M** hopes to become a well-known (and rich) artist.

GIFT Someday, collectors and museums may want to hang my paintings on their walls. I am always hopeful. Nevertheless, I am playing the lottery this week. The jackpot is $20 million and the odds of winning are only 1 in 3 million. I hope the probability is more favorable in the art world.

Above all, avoid the summary ending. Trust your reader to remember the substance of your two- or three-page essay. To say everything again is not only pointless, it borders on being an insult to the reader's intelligence. Your essay isn't a textbook. A chapter review isn't necessary.

Some essays don't need an extended conclusion. When they're over, they're over. Even a short conclusion is better than none at all, however. At the end, readers should feel that they've arrived somewhere. In a sense, every well-planned essay prepares readers for arrival at a certain destination. The introduction tells readers approximately where they're going. En route, a series of ideas propels them toward the conclusion. At the end they're welcomed with a thoughtful gift. When they get to the last word, you don't want readers to say, "Oh, now I see what you've been driving at."

5 REWRITING AND EDITING

This could be the hardest part of writing an essay. You've invested a lot of yourself in the work by this time. You don't want to go back now and start changing things. Who can blame you? Try, however, to resist the impulse to rest. It's not time, yet.

Perhaps you're willing to alter a word here and there, check the spelling, relocate a comma or two and repair a bit of broken-down

Being tough on yourself is a courtesy to your readers.

grammar, but that's proofreading, not rewriting— and it's definitely not enough right now. Proofreading requires skill, but rewriting takes courage. It's painful work, for you may end up discarding large chunks of your essay and rewriting parts you've already rewritten. After you've struggled to get a paragraph just right, it's hard to give it up. Be brave. The next one you write may be even better.

Having Another Look

The root of revision is the word *vision*, that is, sight or perception. When revising, you *look again* to see whether you have said what you intended and arranged your ideas in the best possible order. If you perceive a flaw or weakness, then revise— that is, *rewrite*. Read your essay ten, maybe twenty, times. During each reading, inspect it with a different set of lenses. Read it often for overall impression, but also to check it for each of these qualities:

- **Accuracy.** Have you answered the question on the application?
- **Purpose.** What do you want the reader to think of you after reading the essay? Have you portrayed yourself accurately? Does the essay sound like you?

- **Focus.** Have you limited the subject enough to cover it well in a fairly short essay?
- **Main idea.** What is the point you want to leave in the reader's mind?
- **Unity.** Do you stick to the point from beginning to end? Do you keep reminding the reader of the point? Have you tied ideas together?
- **Organization.** Does your introduction draw readers into the essay? Can you explain the order of ideas in the body of your essay? What does your ending add to the essay?
- **Development.** What is the main point of each paragraph? What does each paragraph contribute to the whole? Have you said enough in each paragraph?

Being tough on yourself is a courtesy to your readers. College admissions officials have plenty to do. You'll spare them extra work by doing all you can to make your writing clear. Readers crave clarity. They want to understand what you say. They won't do your thinking for you, however. Don't assume, "They'll know what I mean." Tell them *exactly* what you mean. By doing so, you'll improve not only the essay but also your chances of getting in.

As you rewrite, deprive the readers of every possible chance to stretch, garble or misconstrue your meaning. Here are some methods you might try:

- *Read your essay aloud. Your ear is a good instrument for detecting words that don't sound right.*
- *Let someone read your essay aloud to you. Listen carefully, and watch his or her face for telltale signs of confusion or doubt.*
- *Let your essay cool for a while—a few hours, a day or so. When you come back, try to read it with the eyes of a stranger.*

The more rewriting you do, the better your essay is likely to be. On the other hand, you could write yourself right out of the essay. Too much painstaking revision may deprive the essay of its personality. The trick is to rewrite repeatedly but to make the words sound natural and spontaneous. Writers work for a long time to perfect the technique.

Finding Your "Voice"

In almost every essay that you're likely to write for a college, a natural, conversational style is appropriate. Since the essay should be personal, the language should sound like you. When you use the pretentious language of a senator, the formal words of a legal document or the slick style of, say, a TV commercial, you're going to sound like a senator, a lawyer or a copy writer, not like yourself.

Don't imitate. Just let your genuine voice ring out.

Don't imitate anyone. Just let your genuine voice ring out. If you think of your writing voice as the sound of your words in a diary or letter to a friend, you'll be getting close. Don't confuse "voice" with speech, however. Voice conveys the personality behind the words. It's not necessary to cram your essay with street talk, half-formed sentences or pop expressions in order to sound real. Rather, consider the voice in your essay as natural speech, shorn of trendy words and expressions, and also grammatically correct, perhaps the casual speech of someone who speaks exceedingly well. As a rule, you might steer clear of writing anything that you'd feel uncomfortable saying aloud in a class discussion or in a friendly conversation with the head of your school.

Question: Can you find Becky's voice in this passage?

> I desire so fervently to attend Amherst because I believe it is the only school that will enable me to explore my intellectual capabilities, heighten my perception of knowledge and gain a greater insight into myself and a greater understanding of others, in an atmosphere of united support for the individual.

No doubt, Becky wants Amherst, but she sounds more like a candidate for public office than a candidate for college. She conceals herself behind high-blown language that may sound important and profound but says very little—very little that's *clear*, at any rate. Contrast this with a passage from Lisa's essay about why she chose Wesleyan:

> During my visit in October, I had a good feeling about the academic life on the campus. It offers so much. I didn't want to go home and back to high school. Everyone I talked to in the dorm seemed happy about being in college there. If I am accepted, I'm sure that I will be bitten by the same bug of enthusiasm.

The voice you hear in Lisa's essay belongs to a genuine person. As she talks, you could be sitting next to her on the bus. Although informal, the writing is controlled.

You hear another kind of voice in this excerpt from the opening of Alec's essay for Columbia:

> You ask me to write an essay about myself. Eh? What can I say? Could Napoleon have written an essay about himself? Oh, what the hell, why not give it a crack, eh what?
>
> When I indulge in one of my favorite activities, thinking about myself, the word *unique* kicks around the old noggin. . . .

Alec sounds like a smart aleck. You'd never guess that he's a deep and discerning thinker. Later in the piece, however, he stops babbling and finds a more honest voice. Breezy it is, but no longer obnoxious:

> Enough about my intellectual musings (and what amusing musings they are). Another field of interest I cultivated in lieu of physical activity was acting. In the 8 years that I have acted professionally, having appeared off Broadway and on a CBS movie of the week, I have basically developed into a character actor. However, I have been working on playing more natural parts lately, and even though I still play character parts, they have become less caricatured and more natural.
>
> Although I intend to pursue acting as a career, I don't intend to major in it. For two reasons: (1) I have other scholarly interests, and (2) I'm a klutz and could never wait on tables to support myself, so I hope to teach instead.

You can check your writing voice by having a friend hand your essay to someone who doesn't know you. If a stranger can describe you accurately after reading your work, you can safely say that you've been faithful to yourself.

Editing for Clarity

You probably started editing your essay soon after composing the first few lines. That is, you changed and reworded sentences to make certain they said what you wanted them to say. As you continue, regard every word and phrase as a potential threat to the clarity of your writing. Ask yourself repeatedly, Is this the clearest word for me to use here? Are these words arranged in the clearest order?

Plain words

To write clearly, use plain words. Never use a complex word because it sounds good or it makes you seem more mature. A college essay is not the place to show off your vocabulary. Use a so-called SAT word only when necessary—that is, when it's

A college essay is not the place to show off your vocabulary.

the only word that will add something to the essay's tone and meaning, which you'll lose by using a common word. Keep that thesaurus on the shelf unless you are stuck. An elegant word used merely to use an elegant word is bombastic . . . er . . . big-sounding and unnatural.

Simple ideas dressed up in ornate words often obscure meaning. Worse, they make the writer sound phony, if not foolish. For example, you wouldn't say, "I'm going to my *domicile*," after a day at school, and you don't call your teachers *pedagogues*. Yet, this overblown sentence appeared on the draft of an essay for Northwestern: "My history pedagogue insisted that I labor in my domicile for 2 hours each night." How much clearer to have written, "My history teacher assigned 2 hours' homework every night."

Notice how clear these sentences sound when the inflated words are removed:

FANCY The more I recalled her degradation of me,
   the more inexorable I became.
PLAIN The more I thought of her insults, the more
   determined I grew.

FANCY During that year, my proclivities toward Italian art were instigated.
PLAIN During that year, I began to favor Italian art.

FANCY I learned the importance of cordiality and cooperation in a competitive racing situation.
PLAIN I learned that teamwork pays off in a race.

Please don't interpret this plea for plain words as an endorsement of current slang. If you need an expression like *air-head, chill* and *pig out,* or a comic-book word like *gonna* and *gotta,* by all means use it. For heaven's sake, though, use such words sparingly and only to create an effect you can't do without. Don't highlight a word with "quotes" to signal that you know it's nonstandard. If to make it's point your essay overdoses on slang, be sure to show your mastery of standard English by writing another part of your application in good, straightforward prose.

English is loaded with simple words that can express the most profound ideas. Descartes' famous observation, "I think. Therefore, I am," reshaped forever the way we think about existence. Descartes may have used esoteric language to make his point, but the very simplicity of his words endows his statement with great power. Ernest Hemingway called a writer's greatest gift a "built-in, shock-proof crap detector." Hemingway's own detector worked well. He produced about the leanest, plainest writing in the English language—not that you should try to emulate Hemingway, although you could do worse, but an efficient crap detector will encourage you to choose words only because they say exactly what you mean.

Exact words

It's often hard to break away from using vague, shadowy, and abstract words. If you want your ideas to sink into the minds of readers, however, give them exact, clear and well-defined words. Almost always, exact words help you express exact thoughts. Since a tight, precise, hard-edged word has an unmistakable meaning, give the reader a *wooden bucket* instead of a *container, a blazing sunset* instead of a *beautiful evening, white-haired and stooped* instead of *old,* and *a Big Mac, large fries and coke* instead of *lunch.*

To write with exact words is to write with pictures, sounds and actions that are as vivid in words as in reality. Exact words hit harder than hazy ones:

HAZY Quite violently, I expressed my anger to the other team's player.
EXACT I punched the Bruins' goalie in the nose and sent him sprawling.

HAZY Skiing is a sport I enjoy, not only for the esthetics, but also for the art and skill involved.
EXACT I like to ski, not just to see snow-decked pines and brilliant sky, but also to weave gracefully down steep slopes.

Of course, you need abstract words, too. Words such as *beauty, love, existence, nobility* and *envy* stand for ideas that exist in the mind. The power to think in terms of *situations, concepts, feelings* and *principles* is unique to humans. An essay full of vague, hard-to-define words and ideas, though, will leave your reader at sea about what you are trying to say. A student who writes about an "ugly" teacher, for example, sends a different image of an ugly person to each reader. If the teacher is *a ragged, slouching beast,* the writer should say so. Or if the teacher's personality is ugly, the student should write *ill-tempered and aloof* or show the teacher shouting harsh threats at the hapless class.

Anticipate reactions to every word. Ask yourself, "Might readers understand this word in any other way than how I meant it?" If so, strike it out and find another.

Although exact words will always be clearer than abstract ones, a word or phrase with multiple meanings may often help to tighten your writing. Every time you mention *dinner,* for example, you need not list the menu. Be aware, though, that nobody will care to read an essay that forgot to come down to earth.

Clear sentences

Short sentences are the clearest—sometimes. Use a short sentence to emphasize a point. Sometimes you may need long sentences to convey complex ideas, although a complex thought may just as easily be expressed in clear, short sentences. When trapped in a long, strung-out sentence, break it into a set of shorter sentences. Later, if necessary, you can put the pieces together again.

Now and then you may run into a long-winded sentence that suffers from paralysis. No matter how you tinker with it you can't make it move without damaging its meaning. Walk away from it and repair it later, or try a few manipulations. Here, to illustrate a stubborn case, is a rambling bit of prose that needs fixing:

A sentence can be molded into almost any shape, beautiful or ugly.

> One of my biggest rewards has been the computer club, which was formed in my junior year, at which time the club members were informed by the computer teacher of a computer contest that was being conducted by Fairfield University.

REMEDY	RESULTS (some better than others)
Break the long sentence into shorter ones.	One of my biggest rewards has been the computer club, which was formed in my junior year. At that time Fairfield University was conducting a computer contest. The computer teacher informed the club members about it. or One of my biggest rewards has been the computer club. It was formed in my junior year. When the club started, the computer teacher informed the members about a computer contest at Fairfield University.
Move words from predicate to subject.	A computer club has been one of my biggest rewards . . .
Combine ideas; turn less important ideas into phrases.	A computer club, formed in my junior year, has been one of my biggest rewards. or Formed in my junior year, a computer club . . .
Change nouns to adjectives.	My most rewarding activity has been a computer club . . .
Change nouns to verbs.	Computer club activities have rewarded me . . .
Change verbs to nouns.	The formation of a computer club . . .
Switch the focus.	A contest at Fairfield University introduced me to the rewards of working with computers . . . or

> My computer teacher introduced me to the most reward-
> ing work. . .
>
> or
>
> I got my start with computers after my teacher. . .

Once you start such sentence manipulations, you may begin to see endless possibilities. A sentence is much like clay. It's malleable and can be molded into almost any shape, beautiful or ugly. In the end the sentence should stand in the form that expresses most clearly and accurately what you want to say.

Clear meaning

In your writing, words must fit together like the pieces of a jigsaw puzzle. Sometimes a word looks as though it fits, but it doesn't. A misplaced word may produce a rather peculiar sentence. Take these, for example:

> While running to English class, the bell rang.
> Working full-time, the summer went by quickly.
> When only 8 years old, my father warned me about smoking.

These may not strike you as funny at first. Look again. Do you see that these sentences describe a weird world in which bells run to class, summers hold full-time jobs, and youthful fathers dispense advice?

The authors of these sentences have tried to join two pieces that don't fit. The grammar is flawless; the spelling and punctuation are perfect. Even the writers' intentions are clear. In each sentence, however, the parts are mismatched. After the comma in each, readers expect to find out who is running, who was working and who is just 8 years old. They don't. They're left dangling. (Hence, the name *dangling modifier* or *dangling participle* has been assigned to this type of sentence construction.)

To keep the reader from dangling, the writers might have said:

> While the boys were running to English class, the bell rang.
> Since Charlotte worked full-time, her summer sped by.
> When I was 8, my father warned me about smoking.

Relative pronouns (*who, whose, whom, that* and *which*) may also lead to problems of clarity. Perhaps such words may not deserve a reputation as troublemakers, but like a black sheep in the family, they have it just the same. They've acquired their name—*relative pronoun*—from their intimate relationship with another word in the same sentence, called an *antecedent.*

A relative pronoun and an antecedent are related because one refers directly to the other. In this sentence,

> It's always my brother who is blamed for trouble in the neighborhood.

the relative pronoun *"who"* and the antecedent *"brother"* are right next to each other, about as close as kin can be. In this sentence,

> It's always my brother, now approaching his twentieth birthday, who is blamed for trouble in the neighborhood.

the phrase *"now approaching his twentieth birthday"* intrudes, thereby weakening the relationship, but the meaning is still clear.

You run into a particular problem with pronouns when you try to establish a tie between the pronoun *which*, for example, and a whole series of actions, feelings or words, as in

> First we had lunch and then our guide told us the secret of the cave, which pleased me.

A reader might honestly wonder what was "pleasing." The cave's secret? The guide's spilling the beans? Lunch? That the secret was revealed after lunch? The pronoun *"which"* might refer to all or to only one of these possible antecedents. It's just not clear. To repair the sentence you might change it into something like this:

> I was pleased that the guide waited until after lunch to tell us the secret of the cave.

If another meaning was intended,

> I was pleased with the secret of the cave, which the guide told us after lunch.

Another sort of pronoun, namely the word *this*, creates similar problems of clarity. Any time you start a sentence with *this*, double-check it. Make sure it refers directly to what you want it to refer. This is advice you should not ignore!

Harmony

Writers, like music makers, strive for harmony in their art. Every chamber ensemble, barbershop quartet and reggae or rock group works hard to achieve a pleasing and unified sound, and you can tell almost instantly whether they've done it. Likewise, when you write an essay you have to work at blending the parts harmoniously. A discordant essay—one in which the pieces seem disconnected—will leave your readers confused.

As you edit your application essay, read it over repeatedly for its internal harmony. That is, check to see if one idea seems to lead naturally and easily to the next. Look for words and phrases that tie ideas together. (Turn to page 63 for some common examples of transitions.) In a harmonious essay, virtually every sentence bears some sort of reference to the sentence that came before. Such references might be obvious, as in "furthermore" or "for example." They are often more subtle, however, as in this pair of sentences:

> I have an idealized image in my mind of families that are
> close, loving, laughing, generous and supportive.
> I wish that I could find *such qualities* in mine.

Notice that the italicized phrase in the second sentence refers directly to adjectives listed in the first.

Sometimes, however, allusions to previous sentences are carried in the meaning rather than by a specific word or phrase:

> I had a hard time finding his house in the dark.
> I *picked out what I thought should be the address* and
> knocked at the front door.

In this example the italicized words establish a link to the idea stated in the first sentence. In the second sentence the speaker feels unsure of an address. You know the reason (because it's dark outside) only because you know what the first sentence says.

Search your essay for transitions of all kinds. Whenever you discover a series of three or more sentences devoid of transitions, you may be stuck with a hard-to-read muddle on your hands. Before you do any heavy rewriting, though, try inserting appropriate transitional words, phrases and sentences. Don't wedge one in where it doesn't belong, however. This could confuse your readers even more.

As you've no doubt realized, editing a piece of writing is a meticulous process. When you examine every word you write, it's easy to drown in a sea of minutiae. Therefore, it helps now and then to stop fussing over the details and to inspect your essay as a whole. Say aloud to yourself or to anyone within earshot, "The point of my essay is. . . ." Complete the statement with one clear, straightforward declarative sentence. If it takes more than a single statement, perhaps your essay isn't sufficiently focused. You may be trying to say more than you have space for.

Now and then, stop fussing over details, and inspect your essay as a whole.

After you've declared your main point, try to say what each part adds to the whole. If any part does not seem to contribute, cast it away. You don't need material that sends readers off the course you've set for them. By attending to the contents of the whole essay, you are in a sense checking its harmony, determining whether all its parts work together in unison.

An outline of your essay will help, too. Such an outline need not follow the formal pattern you may have learned in school, but the same principle applies. That is, all the minor pieces, when added together, should equal the whole. In the language of writers, every sentence in a paragraph supports the main idea of the paragraph, and every paragraph supports the main idea of the essay. You'll know that you have a well-structured, harmonious piece of writing when you can't reasonably remove a piece without causing damage to the whole.

Editing for Interest

Don't bore your readers. Admissions officials may ignore an occasional lapse in clarity and even overlook a flaw in grammar, but if your essay bores them, they'll lose interest in both you and your essay.

Like most applicants, you've probably led a fairly routine life. That's no reason, however, to write a routine essay. Fortunately, there are plenty of techniques for turning an ordinary piece of writing into a highly readable and stylish essay.

Brevity works best

Never use two words when one will do. Readers want to be told quickly and directly what you have to say. Wordiness sucks the life out of your writing. Cut out needless words. Readers value economy.

(Stop! Go back to the last paragraph. Do you see the unnecessary words? Did you notice that the next-to-last sentence reiterates the first? Yes, the statement contains only four words, but are those words necessary? Do they merely add weight—and no substance—to the paragraph?)

Your sentences, like muscles, should be firm and tight. Needless words are flabby. Trim the fat. Make your writing lean. As you edit, exercise your crossing-out muscles.

Go through every sentence and cross out extra words. The sentence you just read contains nine words (forty-three letters). It could be trimmed still more. For example, "Cut extra words out of every sentence" (seven words, thirty-one letters). When the sentence was first written, it read, "The writer should work through all the sentences he writes by examining each one and crossing out all the extra words" (twenty-one words, ninety-seven letters)—three times longer than the trim, seven-word model, and three times duller.

In lean writing every word counts. One missing word distorts or changes the meaning. To trim your sentences, squeeze them through your fat detector.

1. Look for repetition. Then combine sentences.

    FAT In tenth grade I accepted a position at Wilkins' Fabrics. In this position I learned about fabrics and about how to handle customers. (23 words)

TRIMMED In tenth grade I accepted a position at Wilkins' Fabrics, where I learned about fabrics and handling customers. (18)

RETRIMMED Working at Wilkins' Fabrics since tenth grade, I have learned to handle both fabrics and customers. (16)

2. Look for telltale words like *which, who, that, thing* and *all.* They may indicate the presence of fat.

FAT Manicotti is a dish *that* I always enjoy eating. (9)
TRIMMED I like manicotti any time. (5)

FAT Jogging has been a wonderful activity, *which* has stimulated my body and freed my mind to think. (17)
TRIMMED Jogging has been wonderful for stimulating my body and freeing my mind. (12)

FAT The *thing* that made me angry was mosquitoes inside my shirt. (11)
TRIMMED Mosquitoes inside my shirt angered me. (6)

3. Look for phrases that add words but little meaning.

FAT *At this point in time,* I am not able to say. (11)
TRIMMED I can't say now. (4)

FAT The chef stayed home *as a result of* his not feeling well. (12)
TRIMMED The chef stayed home because he felt sick. (8)

—A baker's dozen specially selected fat phrases—
No, make that *thirteen selected fat phrases:*

FAT	TRIMMED
what I mean is	I mean
after all is said and done	finally
for all intents and purposes	(omit)
in the final analysis	finally
few and far between	few
each and every one	each
this is a subject that	this subject
ten in number	ten
at the age of 6 years old	at age 6
most unique	unique
true fact	fact
biography of his life	biography
in regard to, with regard to, in relation to, with reference to	about

Readers are too busy for sentences stuffed with fat phrases.

After your sentences are pared to the bone, look at what remains and get ready to cut some more. Although it hurts to take out what you worked hard to put in, the writing will be stronger, more readable and noticeably more interesting.

Show, don't tell

T he genius who invented "show and tell" realized that seeing a pet frog or a souvenir model of Grant's Tomb was far more interesting to an audience than just hearing about it. Since writers can't use hands, make faces or dangle an object in front of readers, writers must rely on words to do both the telling and the showing.

Show more than you tell. Use words to make the reader *see*.

Show more than you tell. Use words to make the reader *see*. For example, don't leave the reader guessing about Laura's beautiful hair. *Show* how the breeze catches the edge of her silky, brown hair. Don't just tell about the garbage in the hallway. *Show* the splintered glass lying in the oily water, the half-torn notebook and the newspaper, yellowed with age. Don't just say you felt happy. *Show* yourself bounding down the steps four at a time, coat unzipped, shouting into the wind, "Hurray, I did it!"

TELL After I won, I experienced a wonderful and unique feeling which makes me want to win again.

SHOW After I won, my sense of accomplishment grew with every handshake and pat on the back. My face ached from grinning so much. I knew that I'd be back next year to win again.

TELL There is so much I have to do after school that I often don't even have time for homework.

SHOW The busy part of my life starts at three o'clock: pick up Scott, my baby brother, piano lessons on Tuesdays at four, French Club and work on the newspaper, tutoring my neighbor in math. I don't have time for homework, not to speak of my Jane Fonda workout.

When words show what you have in mind, the reader can see and feel and hear what you saw and felt and heard. It takes details—lots and lots of them—to make a sight or sound or smell as real for the reader as it is for you.

Your essay would soon grow tedious—both to write and to read—

if you showed every grain of sand on the beach. Be selective. Show readers the sights you want them to *see:* the gleaming sand and fragments of clam shells; to *hear:* the squawk of gulls and children's shouts; to *smell:* salt spray, seaweed and suntan oil; to *feel:* stinging feet and sweaty, sun-baked backs; and to *taste:* gritty egg-salad sandwiches and parched, salt-caked lips.

Although too much detail can be boring, too little is just as bad. A balance is best. No one can tell you exactly how to achieve that balance. You need time to get the feel of it. Like walking a tightrope, riding a bike or doing a back flip, it becomes instinct after a while. The context, as well as your judgment of the reader's intelligence, will have to determine how detailed you need to be. To get the knack a little more quickly, study a written passage that you found interesting. Pick out both details and broad statements. Use the passage as a general model for your own writing, but give it your own stamp. After all, it's your voice the reader wants to hear.

Active verbs

At some point you must have learned that a verb is a word that shows *action or state of being.* That's a fair description of a verb if you're learning grammar. To an essay writer, however, knowing that *action* verbs differ from *being* verbs is far more impor-

Active verbs pump life into your writing.

tant. You need active verbs to stimulate interest. Since active verbs describe or show movement, they create life. They perform, stir up, get up and move around. They excel all other words in their power to pump vitality into your writing. They add energy and variety to sentences. As a bonus, active verbs often help you trim needless words from your writing.

In contrast, being verbs are stagnant. They don't do anything. Notice the lifelessness in all the most common forms of the verb *to be: is, are, was, were, am, has been, had been, will be.* When used in a sentence, each of these being verbs joins the subject to the predicate—and that's all. In fact, the verb *to be* acts much like an equals sign in an equation, as in "Four minus three is one" ($4 - 3 = 1$), "Harold is smart" (Harold = smart), or "That is some spicy meatball" (That = SSMB). Because equals signs (and being verbs) show no action, use active verbs whenever you can.

Being verbs are perfectly acceptable in speech and writing. In fact, it's hard to get along without them. Be stingy, however. If more than, say, one-fourth of your sentences use a form of *to be* as the main verb, perhaps you're relying too heavily on being verbs.

Substitute active verbs for being verbs by extracting them from other words in the same sentence. For instance,

BEING VERB Linda was the winner of the raffle.
ACTIVE VERB Linda won the raffle.

Here the verb *"won"* has been extracted from the noun *"winner."*
Active verbs may also be extracted from adjectives, as in:

BEING VERB My summer at the New Jersey shore was
enjoyable.
ACTIVE VERB I enjoyed my summer at the New Jersey shore.

Sometimes it pays to substitute an altogether fresh verb:

BEING VERB It is not easy for me to express my feelings.
ACTIVE VERB I find it difficult to express my feelings.

BEING VERB There was a distant wailing of an ambulance.
ACTIVE VERB We heard the distant wailing of an
ambulance.

Practice will help you purge being verbs from your sentences and add
vitality to whatever you write.

The noun you employ as the subject of a sentence will often
determine your chances of using a lively verb. Abstract nouns limit
your opportunities. For example, you're almost compelled to use a
form of *to be* in any sentence that begins with *"The reason,"* as in
"The reason I am applying to Colgate is." You have few verb choices,
too, when the subject of the sentence is *thought, concept, idea, issue,
way, cause* or any other abstract noun.

On the other hand, nouns that stand for specific people, places,
events and objects take active verbs easily. When your sentence contains a subject that can do something—a person, for instance—you
can choose from among thousands of active verbs. Anytime you
replace a general or abstract noun with a solid, easy-to-define noun,
you are likely to end up with a tight, energetic, generally more
interesting sentence:

ABSTRACT SUBJECT The issue was settled by Mrs.
Marino.
DEFINITE SUBJECT Mrs. Marino settled the issue.

ABSTRACT SUBJECT The cause of the strike was the
students' demand for peace.
DEFINITE SUBJECT The students struck for peace.

ABSTRACT SUBJECT The way to Memorial Hospital
is down this road.
DEFINITE SUBJECT This road goes to Memorial
Hospital.

Being verbs aren't alone in their dullness. They share that dis-
tinction with *have, come, go, make, move* and *get*. These common

verbs do little to enliven writing. Each has so many different uses that they creep into sentences virtually unnoticed. Use them freely in contexts where they fit, of course, but stay alert for more vivid and lively substitutes.

Active sentences

Most events in life don't just occur by themselves. Somebody does something, somebody *acts*. Hamburgers don't just get eaten. People—Julie, Paul and Mr. Dolan—eat them. Marriages don't just happen; men and women deliberately go out and marry each other. Touchdowns don't score, jails don't just fill up, graves aren't dug, cotton isn't picked and herring do not simply get caught and stuffed into jars. People do all these things.

To create interest, take advantage of your readers' natural curiosity about others.

The deeds that people do register quickly on a reader's mind. To create interest in your writing, therefore, take advantage of your reader's natural curiosity about others. Always write active sentences. Even those sentences in which no specific action occurs can be written in an "active," rather than a "passive," voice.

For example, consider who performed an action in this sentence:

> Six nights a week were spent in preparation for the concert by our class.

Clearly, the class acted. More precisely, it rehearsed for a concert, but the sentence kept you waiting until the end to tell you who performed an action. Moreover, by placing "our class" at the end, the writer has been obliged to use the passive verb, *"were spent."* If you relocate "our class" to the beginning of the sentence, you suddenly activate the whole statement:

> Our class rehearsed six nights a week in preparation for the concert.

The change not only tightens and enlivens the sentence, it adds interest. You derive the same results any time you turn passive sentences into active ones:

PASSIVE Every day, the newspaper was brought home by my father.

ACTIVE My father brought home the newspaper every day.

PASSIVE Rutgers was attended by my brother, my cousin and three of my uncles.

ACTIVE My brother, my cousin and three uncles went to Rutgers.

Although active sentences are usually more natural, compact and interesting, sometimes to avoid awkwardness you may need to use the passive voice. When you are uncertain who performed an action, for instance, or when it isn't important to say:

PASSIVE The blue curtain was raised at 8:30.
ACTIVE At 8:30, a stagehand (or Mary Ann, a production assistant) raised the curtain.

In the passive sentence curtain time is the important fact. Who pulled the rope is immaterial.

Fresh language and surprises

Fresh language (1) stimulates the mind, (2) pleases the ear, and (3) surprises the emotions—all praiseworthy effects of a college essay. Dull writing, on the other hand, is predictable. That is, you can almost tell what word is likely to come next in a sentence. When readers know what to expect, they'll soon lose interest, both in the writing and its author. If you serve up verbal surprises, however, your readers will stick with you.

When you surprise your readers, they'll stick with you.

You don't need rare or unusual words to surprise your readers. A common word, deftly used, will do:

ORDINARY I was ten before I saw my first pigeon.
SURPRISING I was ten before I met my first pigeon.

Since people don't normally *meet* pigeons, the unexpected shift from *saw* to *met* creates a small surprise.

ORDINARY The shark bit the swimmers.
SURPRISING The shark dined on the swimmers.

Changing the verb *bit* to *dined* makes a common sentence uncommon, because the word *dined* suggests good manners and gentility, pleasures that few sharks enjoy.

Sounds can create surprises, too. Some words match the sounds they describe. The word *bombard*, for example, makes a heavy, explosive sound. *Yawn* has a wide-open sound that can be stretched out indefinitely. *Choke* sticks in your throat. *Murmuring streams* evokes the sound of—what else?

A reader often derives unexpected pleasure from the repetition of sounds—either consonants or vowels—as in "The dark, dank day smelled of death" or "The machine sucked up the sewage in the swamp." You probably shouldn't repeat sounds too often because they may distract the reader from the meaning of your words, but an occasional treat for the ear builds interest in your writing.

Surprise with comparisons

I t isn't easy to find just the right word to express all you think, sense and do. How, for instance, do you show the look a toll collector gave you, or how do you describe six-in-the-morning street sounds? What about the taste of stale Coke, the smell of marijuana, the feel of clean sheets, a fear, a frustration?

With comparisons you can express the inexpressible.

Writers often catch those elusive details and fleeting sensations by making comparisons. An original comparison will not only delight your reader, but it will provide you with words to express your most inexpressible ideas. In addition, comparisons are economical. They require fewer words than you might otherwise need to state an idea.

To describe old men in a nursing home, for instance, you could show their creased faces, the folds of papery skin at their throats, the pale, cracked lips and the white stubble on their chins. If you don't need all those details in your essay, you could simply compare the men to slats on weathered wooden fence. Instantly your reader will get the picture. Yes, the rough gray texture of weather-beaten boards does suggest withered men lined up in a nursing home corridor, a likeness that probably hadn't occurred to the reader before.

Small children usually don't know enough words to express all they want to say. By nature, therefore, they make comparisons: "Daddy, when my foot goes to sleep, it feels like ginger ale." As people get older, they often lose the knack and have to relearn it. When you consciously seek comparisons, though, you'll find them sprouting everywhere—like weeds. Compare, for example, the taste of fruit punch to antifreeze, a sweet look to something you'd pour on waffles, a friend's voice to a chicken's cackle, the smell of a locker room to rotting hay.

Figures of speech, such as similes (Tom wrestles *like* a tiger) and metaphors (Tom *is* a tiger), are types of comparisons. They help the writer point out likenesses between something familiar (tiger) and something unfamiliar (Tom the wrestler). One side of the comparison must always be common and recognizable. Therefore, comparing the cry of the Arctic tern to the song of a tree toad won't help a reader familiar with neither water birds nor tree toads. Since most people know what a fiddle sounds like, a more revealing comparison would be: *The cry of the Arctic tern sounds like a fiddler tuning up.*

American English is littered with hundreds of metaphors and similes, once fresh and surprising, but now dried out and lifeless. Avoid those like the plague. "*Like the plague,*" in fact, is one you should avoid. Figures of speech like "*high as a kite*" and "*pale as a ghost*" have lost their zing. Don't resurrect them in your essay. Let them rest in the cliché graveyard.

At one time, every familiar combination of words, such as *"you've got to be kidding"* and *"I could care less"* was new, witty or poetic. Such expressions were so striking that people, thinking that they would seem up-to-date, witty or poetic, used them over and over. Constant use dulled them and turned them into clichés. No reader will delight in a cliché. By definition, a cliché has lost its kick.

A treasury of worthless phrases and expressions to be avoided *at all costs*

bummer
how does that sit with you?
to touch base with
off the top of my head
try an idea on for size
how does that grab you?
that's beat!
far out!
I'm getting psyched

would you believe?
go off the deep end
have a fit
for openers
flipped out
get off my back
super!
so amazing
no way

There are countless others to guard against. The number is *awesome.* They sneak into writing *when your back is turned,* when *your defenses are down,* and *when you least expect them.* Beware!

To avoid overused expressions, ask yourself whether you've ever heard or seen the phrase before. If you have, drop it, not *like a hot potato,* but just as quickly.

Sentence variety

Monotony kills interest. A steady diet of mashed potatoes dulls the taste buds. A 200-mile stretch on a straight road takes the joy out of driving. Day after day of routine rots the brain. Listening too often to the same song destroys its charm. So it is with writing an essay. Repetition of the same sentence pattern makes readers wish they didn't have to read any further. Keep your readers awake, alert and interested by serving up a variety of sentence patterns.

Sentence variety keeps readers awake, alert, and interested.

Most English sentences begin with the subject, as in

My sister got married last summer in a hot-air balloon 1000 feet over Connecticut.

To avoid the monotony of many successive sentences in the same pattern, move the subject elsewhere and look for other ways to start a sentence:

In a hot-air balloon 1000 feet over Connecticut, my sister married her high school sweetheart Jack.

After an initial prepositional phrase, the writer named the subject, "*my sister.*"

> Surprisingly, ten people witnessed the wedding—five in the same balloon basket, and five in another.

Obviously, the writer began this sentence with an adverb.

> When word got out about the wedding site, reporters hounded the couple for days.

After introducing this sentence with a dependent clause, the writer named the subject, "*reporters,*" and then added the rest of the sentence.

> Still, the ceremony itself was held without fanfare.

This writer snuck in the subject after an opening connective.

> To keep the wedding quiet, Jack and Annie kept the date to themselves until the night before the flight.

To compose this sentence, the writer began with a *verbal*, in this instance the infinitive form of the verb *keep*. Verbals look and feel like verbs, but aren't. At least they're not the verbs that groups of words need to qualify as complete sentences. Verbals come from verbs, though, which explains the resemblance.

> Drinking champagne, the guests flew for an hour before landing on a par-four fairway of a golf course.

Hoping to keep the reader's interest, this writer began the sentence with another kind of verbal—a participle. Very often the *i-n-g* ending indicates that you've used a participle.

> Thrilled by the adventure, the wedding party vowed to fly again on Jack and Annie's first anniversary.

Determined to begin a sentence with another kind of verbal, the writer chose a verb with an *e-d* ending, which functions like an adjective.

Still another appealing variation is the sentence containing a paired construction. In such a sentence, you have two equal and matched ideas. Sometimes the ideas differ only by one or two words, as in: "*It wasn't that I was turning away from my family, it was my family that was turning away from me*" or "*While I put my heart into dancing, dancing worked its way into my heart.*" The strength of such sentences lies in the balance of parallel parts. Each part could stand alone, but together the thought becomes memorable.

Once in a great while, you can create interest by reversing the usual order of words in a sentence. When used often the writing will sound stilted and unnatural, but look at the power you get out of a sentence that begins with an adjective that you want the reader to remember: "*Desperate I grew when the telegram hadn't arrived.*" Likewise, an inverted statement—"*A math genius I am not*"—carries a lot more punch than "*I am not a math genius.*" Use inverted sentences cautiously, though. In the wrong place they'll sound silly.

Lucky is the writer in search of variety, for English contains a huge selection of sentence types, many of which you probably learned about in school. Obviously, there are long and short sentences. At your fingertips you also have simple, compound and complex sentences. You have declarative, interrogative, imperative and exclamatory sentences. You can write sentences interrupted in midstream by a dash—although some people will tell you it's not quite proper. You can also use direct and indirect quotes, and once in a great while—to drive home a point—a single emphatic word. Perfect!

With such an array, there's no excuse for writing humdrum sentences that march monotonously through your essay. Please your reader with combinations and variations. Don't mix up sentence types just to mix up sentence types, however. You may end up with a mess on your hands. Always be guided by what seems clearest and by what seems varied enough to hold your reader's interest.

A note on repetition

n occasion, skillful use of repetition enables you to stress an idea in an unusual way. At first glance, for example, this passage from **Sally McC'**s essay appears repetitive:

> My grandmother raised me. She took pride in her five grandchildren. She introduced me to theater and ballet. She sat patiently through my piano and dance recitals. She sent me to sleep-away camp every summer. She did all a mother is expected to do except live long enough to see me applying to Smith, her alma mater.

Every sentence but the first starts with the same word. Yet, the paragraph isn't monotonous. What strikes you is not the similarity of the sentences, but the grandmother's devotion to child rearing. In this instance, Sally used repetition to her advantage.

Short and long sentences

Sentences come in all lengths, from one word to thousands. A long sentence demands greater effort from readers because, while stepping from one part of the sentence to the next, they must keep track of more words, modifiers, phrases (not to speak

A balance of short and long sentences works best.

of parenthetical asides) and clauses without losing the writer's main thought, which may be buried amid any number of secondary, or less important, thoughts. Short sentences are easier to grasp. A brief sentence makes its point quickly and sometimes with considerable potency, as for example in this passage from **Tracy P**'s essay about a trip to Florida:

> For a day and a night the five of us—my parents, two sisters and I—sat upright in our van and drove and drove and drove. For 30 hours we shared our thoughts and dreams, counted McDonalds, told stories, ate granola bars, drank juice, dozed, played twenty questions, sat wordlessly and finally, by the water in Daytona, we watched a brilliant crimson sun rise out of the Atlantic. But mostly, we argued.

The brief sentence at the end jolts the reader. Its bluntness, especially after a windy, forty-two-word sentence, produces a mild shock. Placing a tight, terse sentence next to a lengthy one creates a startling effect. The technique, however, works best when used only rarely. Overuse dilutes its impact.

Also, several short sentences in a row can be as tiresome as a string of long, complex sentences. A balance works best. If you have strung together four or five equally long (or short) sentences, separate (or combine) them. Here, to illustrate, is a drawn-out sentence in need of dismemberment:

> Because I was certain that it would be all right, without waiting for the approval of my mother, who was not yet home from the hospital after her operation for a back ailment that had been troubling her for years—in fact, ever since her automobile accident on the way to Chicago one Christmas, I decided during spring vacation to apply for a job as a counsellor at a summer camp for children, 6 to 14 years old, in Brookdale, a tiny village close to my uncle's farm in Wisconsin.

To lighten the load of an extended sentence like this, you could divide it, rearrange it, add verbs, drop an idea or two, change the emphasis and excise words. You could employ some of the sentence-fixing tools described on pages 87 to 89. When you're done, the ideas, now clearer and more streamlined, might sound something like this:

> During spring vacation I applied for a counsellor's job at a summer camp in the tiny village of Brookdale, Wisconsin. The camp, for 6- to 14-year-olds, is near my uncle's farm. I was certain my mother wouldn't mind. So I didn't wait for her return from the hospital, where she was recuperating from an operation for a back ailment.

Conversely, you achieve greater balance when you combine a string of several very short sentences. For instance:

> I live in two environments. I was born in Canada. I lived there for 10 years. Then we moved to Boston. That was an important event. It was painful. The kids in Boston were cold and distant. All my friends were in Montreal.

Although the terse sentences may vaguely suggest the writer's despair, the writing style calls to mind a grade school primer. Greater fluidity and grace are expected from college applicants. Therefore, a renovation of the passage is needed—perhaps something like this:

> I am from two environments, one Canadian and one American. I was born in Montreal, but moved to Boston at age 10. The move was painful. Cold and distant acquaintances surrounded me in Boston. Friends lived in Montreal.

Note that you frequently get a small bonus when you combine sentences: Your writing gets more active and less wordy—both worthy goals for a writer.

The final check

I f you took the task of editing seriously, your essay should now be in very good shape, maybe in better shape than you are. Many writers, even the best, sometimes don't know whether their hard labor and sacrifice are worth it. They can't tell whether they've done a good job. Self-doubt is the writer's trademark, the price you pay for a clear, precise, interesting and correct essay.

Although your essay may half-sicken you by now, stick with it just a little longer. It's probably better than you think. After all, you're not a professional writer so you shouldn't expect to write like one. High school quarterbacks don't play for the Giants, high school actors don't win Emmies and high school writers—even the best of them—can't compete with the professionals. Chances are you've written a decent essay that will stand up in any college admissions office. Your struggle to get the words right has probably paid off. You've revised and edited, re-revised and re-edited. Good! You added, cut, switched parts around. Very good! That shows you've been thinking. You used up lots of paper. You walked away, came back, tried again. Perhaps you wrote ten times as many words as you actually used.

Finally, you got the words the way you wanted them—the way they should be. You survived the ordeal, and the reader in the admissions office, who doesn't know you yet—but soon will—will be happy to make your acquaintance.

Before you type the finished copy of your essay, check the whole thing one more time. Don't be satisfied until you can answer YES! to all the questions on this **Editing Checklist:**

	YES!	MOSTLY	HARDLY	NO
Does the essay *sound* like you?	☐	☐	☐	☐
Have you used *plain* words?	☐	☐	☐	☐
Have you used *exact* language?	☐	☐	☐	☐
Does your essay have *focus*?	☐	☐	☐	☐
Are all parts in *harmony*?	☐	☐	☐	☐
Is each sentence *accurately* worded?	☐	☐	☐	☐
Have you *trimmed* needless words?	☐	☐	☐	☐

	YES!	MOSTLY	HARDLY	NO
Do you *show* more than *tell?*	☐	☐	☐	☐
Have you used *active verbs?*	☐	☐	☐	☐
Is your language *fresh?*	☐	☐	☐	☐
Do you include verbal *surprises?*	☐	☐	☐	☐
Are your sentences *varied?*	☐	☐	☐	☐
Is sentence length *balanced?*	☐	☐	☐	☐

6 PRESENTING *YOUR* ESSAY

Appearance

Would you like to hear a sad but true story? It's about Robert, a high school senior, a good student with a keen desire to go to Amherst. He wrote his essay with care but sent it in looking as though it had been stored in his jeans for a week. Robert was rejected. The admissions people concluded that Robert couldn't be seriously interested in Amherst if he submitted such a sloppy-looking piece of work.

Obviously, there's a lesson in Robert's tale: Don't send in an essay that looks anything less than gorgeous.

Present your essay with pride. That is, make it neat, crisp, easy to read, accurately typed, in all respects as close to perfect as it can be. Its appearance speaks for you as clearly as its content. As Jonathan H. Henry, assistant director of admissions at the University of Vermont, observes, "Your essay should look like your laundry—clean, without spots and freshly washed."

> **"Your essay should be like your laundry—clean, without spots and freshly washed."**

Unless the college asks for an essay written in your own hand, as Brown University does, type it, preferably on an electric or electronic typewriter with a fresh ribbon. A word processor is fine, too, provided that your printer is letter-quality or close to it. Dot-matrix type is often hard to read unless the ribbon is brand new. A handwritten essay needs to be as legible as you can make it. If your script is flawed, then print. Keep a bottle of correction fluid handy. In short, do all you can to make your essay easy on the eyes.

Use high-quality white paper, 8½ by 11 inches. Separate continuous computer paper into sheets, and remove the perforated edges.

Double-space for ease of reading. Center the text on the page, and leave at least a 1-inch margin all around. Number your pages. If you're asked to write more than one essay, designate which is which with the question number or topic on the application.

Many colleges give you a word limit. They mean business, so stick to the number of words they ask for. It's permissible to go over or under by, say, 10 percent. More will count against you. Some applications provide a few inches of space for your answer. Rather than fill up every square millimeter with type or minuscule writing, cut words from your piece. What you may lose in content, you'll make up in legibility. In a pinch, you can reduce the size of your type with a photocopying machine and glue the reduced version neatly onto the application.

It goes without saying that cross-outs and last-minute insertions using arrows, asterisks, paragraph markers or carets are not acceptable. Don't change anything on your final copy unless you are prepared to retype the whole page. Aim to make your essay letter-perfect. In all respects, neatness counts.

Proofreading

To proofread well, you need fresh eyes. Therefore, your best proofreading method is to let someone else do it. Photocopy five copies of your essay, and have five reliable readers scour your piece for flaws in grammar, punctuation and spelling.

If you're on your own, put your essay aside for a few days, if possible. Then read your essay slowly, once for the sense of it and once for mechanics. Read it a line at a time, keeping a hawklike watch on every letter, word and mark of punctuation. You might even cut a narrow horizontal window out of a spare sheet of paper. Move the window over your essay a line at a time. Concentrate on that line only, reading it once forward and once back. On the backward reading you'll lose the sense of the meaning, allowing you to keep your mind on the spelling.

Read your essay slowly, once for the sense of it and once for the mechanics.

Pay particular attention to words that sound alike but take different spellings: *there, their* and *they're, its* and *it's, to, two* and *too.* Also such words as *principal* and *principle, stationery* and *stationary, whether* and *weather* and the dozens of other homonymns that trap unwary writers. Watch out also for commonly misspelled demons like *a lot, all right, already, separate, doesn't, should've* and of course, *hemorrhoids.* Keep a dictionery at your elbow as you proofread!

Getting Help

Since you began your essay, it's likely that you've shown drafts to people you trust—good friends, a parent, teacher, advisor or college counselor. When you're facing a tough new assignment like writing a college essay, it's natural to seek a word of encouragement or help. Indeed, you're lucky to know people who will help. Getting help from others, though, raises the impossible ethical question: When does your work cease to be yours and become theirs? There's a thin boundary between help and meddling. With luck, your well-meaning helpers haven't overstepped it.

> **It's immoral and dangerous to submit an essay that cannot honestly be called yours.**

If you've received suggestions for rewording a sentence or two, changing a few words or clarifying an idea, you are probably still master of your own essay. If the help consisted of extensive rewriting, bloodying your paper with a river of red ink, and putting words in your mouth, you're about to submit an essay that cannot honestly be called yours. This is not only immoral, it's dangerous.

"One of the best pieces of prose I've seen so far may not have been written by the applicant," says Dean Henry F. Bedford of the Amherst admissions office. Even though Bedford couldn't prove the essay had been ghostwritten, the applicant was turned down. With a huge pool of irreproachable candidates, Amherst didn't need or want to take a chance.

People who read college essays for a living know the distinctive style of high school writing. Even the best of it differs from the writing of adults. Perhaps it's the rhythm, the use of a certain word, an unusual turn of phrase, the juxtaposition of ideas—each can tip off a reader that an adult has had a hand in the essay. There are certain usages that, although natural for an experienced adult writer, would almost never find their way into a high school student's essay. (The sentence you just read contains just such an example. Notice that the subordinate clause, "although natural for an experienced adult writer," is embedded in the main clause. One in a thousand high school writers is likely to construct a sentence like that. It would be equally rare, too, for a high school student to say "usages . . . find their way". Teenagers don't express themselves that way.)

That's not to say that every ably written application essay will arouse suspicion in the admissions office. Many applicants write superior essays all by themselves. If a student with average English grades and unexceptional College Board scores submits a slick, highly sophisticated essay, however, a reader will notice. When admissions officers have reason to question the authorship of an essay, they'll scrutinize the applicant's school record and search through teachers' recommendations for mention of the student's writing ability. If they still have doubts, they may phone the high school for verification.

In recent years, applicants from certain regions of the country started sending in well-polished essays in large numbers. Wondering what caused the change, colleges soon discovered that many high schools had made instruction in application essay writing a part of the curriculum. They also found that teachers, writers and counselors, calling themselves "college consultants" or "education specialists," were giving more than casual lessons in essay writing. For up to $100 an hour, some consultants were all but composing essays for anxious students. Parents, hoping to gain an edge in the competition for hot colleges, were gladly paying the fees. A short time later, some colleges began to ask applicants whether they received professional help in completing their applications. In general, colleges take a dim view of students who seek outside aid in writing application essays. Given a choice between two equally qualified candidates, a college will favor the student who wrote the essay without coaching from a professional.

As consultants flourish, college officials are considering what to do next about applicants from privileged places like Scarsdale, Greenwich and Beverly Hills. "Maybe we won't use the essay so much in the future," says assistant director of admissions Karen W. Ley of Lafayette College. Instead, other information about a candidate will carry greater weight. In 1988, Middlebury College expects to drop the application essay altogether.

Getting substantial help with an essay may reduce your anxiety, but it also does you a disservice. You should make it into the college of your choice based on what you know, what you can do and who you are. Misrepresenting yourself may get you in, but once on campus you will do the work, you will do the writing, you will sink or swim on your own. An essay that fools the admissions office will grant you a short-lived victory. In a few months, the real you will start bringing home real grades. Your application essay will be history, as will, perhaps, your career as a student at that college.

In Addition to Your Essay

Some colleges want more than an essay from you. They ask for paragraph-long responses to any number of questions—why you chose that particular college, which extracurricular activity you like the most, your favorite book, career plans, honors and so on. Whatever your answers, write them with the same care as your essay. Start with drafts. Revise and edit. Use your most interesting writing style. Since you're usually limited to less than half a dozen lines, get to the point promptly and express yourself concisely. Be attentive to the sound and appearance of your responses.

Some questions invite you to reply with a list of some kind—travels, prizes, alumni connections. If you can, however, respond with a thoughtful, well-developed paragraph. Not only will your answer be more interesting to read, you'll have the opportunity to highlight the items that matter. Moreover, the reader will note that you took the trouble to write a coherent, lucid paragraph and that your writing repertoire contains more than just a college essay.

When an application asks, "Is there additional information we should know?" try to reply with an emphatic "Yes!" Since your essay won't have told them everything, grab this chance to explain more of yourself or to show your interests and accomplishments. Applicants frequently send their creative work—perhaps a short story, a collection of poetry, articles written for the school paper, slides of artwork, photographs—almost anything that fits into an envelope or small package. Don't overdo it, though. One carefully chosen term paper will suffice to reveal your love of history. One chapter of your novel is more than admissions people will have time to read, anyway. Quality, not quantity, counts.

Whatever you send, prepare it with the same high standards you used on your essay. Written material should be typed, photographs and artwork should be attractively displayed and clearly explained or captioned. Before you mail a tape of your music or a video of your gymnastic performance, wind it to the starting spot. Make certain that it works and that it contains only what you want the college to hear or see. Also, submit only a few minutes' worth of material—not your whole concert or routine.

Don't feel obliged to create a piece of work just for your college application. Most people don't. It's not their style. "I would hate for

Don't go too far trying to be clever. Being yourself is your best bet.

people to get the idea that they *have* to do something," says Northwestern's director of undergraduate admissions, Carol Lunkenheimer. If you can do or show something that displays your uniqueness, though, by all means use it. For example, a girl, interested in photography, included a male pinup calendar she and a friend had marketed. "It was in good taste and well done," said Claudia Miller, an admissions counselor at Ohio Wesleyan. A young man who makes and sells intricate metal puzzles sent one to Ohio Wesleyan's Fred Weed to play with. Two friends, both applying to Columbia, sent in a movie they had made together. One aspiring architect submitted his blueprints for a geodesic-domed city with his MIT application. The Northwestern admissions office received a poem written on a jigsaw puzzle. To read the poem, the puzzle had to be assembled. It's not clear, however, whether it was ever completed.

Be creative, of course. Be serious if you're serious, witty if you're witty. Just don't go too far trying to be clever. Being yourself is your best bet.

Your Friend, the Mail Carrier

What a glorious feeling it will be to turn your application and essay over to the U.S. Postal Service. Before you do, however, make photocopies. Once in the mail, you'll never see them again. Then sit back and rejoice. Pat yourself on the back for a job well done. Relax and wait for the momentous day when the postman brings you the *fat* envelope—the one containing information about housing, courses, freshman orientation and, of course, the letter that begins, "It gives me great pleasure to tell you that you have been accepted in the class of . . . ."

APPENDIX A. ESSAYS IN PROGRESS

En route from first to final draft, essay writers often pause to survey the progress they've made. After writing each draft, they decide whether to continue as before, alter their course or even start all over again. This appendix contains two sample essays somewhere on the journey to completion. Each draft is followed by notes on what the writer should do next. Notice that later drafts of each essay incorporate the suggestions for improvement. With more drafts, who knows—the writers may have produced essays to stir the blood of the most hard-hearted admissions dean.

Larry H's First Draft

Larry wrote his first draft rather quickly—and it shows. The basic premise of his essay, though, is clever. The piece is written from the point of view of a stranger who has stumbled upon Larry's journal, reads it and draws some inferences about its author.

When a person reads my journal he'll have the impression that this person named Larry H is a pretty good guy. He has his head together and his family is quite closely knit together. His father, who is a lawyer, and his mother, who works in a theater agency, both have jobs in the city. His house sounds like there's more going on there than there is at a three-ring circus.

The person who reads the journal will also notice that Larry likes to make a lot of observations of the life around him and that he states how he gets affected by the things happening around him. Even if he has a problem, somehow he'll work everything out and everything will be all right again. He also likes to question things, and he wonders about the big philosophical questions about the meaning of life.

One nice thing about him is that it seems like he is really close to all his brothers and his father and mother, and he is very much affected by what goes on in his family.

It also says that he likes to watch movies and also that he doesn't go to the movies just to go out. He comments on what the movie means to him, and he likes to analyze the filmmaker's techniques. All in all, what the person will see is a young man who is very humorous and sensitive.

Notes to Larry

■ *You think highly of yourself. You seem self-confident. You take pride in your family and appear to enjoy life. That's good, because colleges like upbeat personalities.*

■ *Maintain the premise of your piece—that is, what a stranger might say about you after reading your journal. The point of view is unconventional and will set your essay apart from others. You might try to let us hear directly from the stranger. What would he actually say about Larry H?*

■ *You have lots of ideas. Too many, in fact, because your essay lacks focus. Concentrate on one important aspect of your life: your family, perhaps, or going to the movies, or your strong sense of self.*

■ *You rely too heavily on generalizations. Use vivid examples that show your humor and show the three-ring circus at your house. What are "things happening around him?" Be more specific. Use the word thing less frequently.*

■ *Think about organization, and keep related parts together. Notice that you discuss your family in both the first and third paragraphs.*

■ *You use too many compound sentences. Greater sentence variety will create more interest.*

Larry's Second Draft

Walking home from school today, I found a notebook on the sidewalk. I took it home and looked inside it. It turned out to be a journal that belonged to someone named Larry H. Since I had nothing better to do, I decided to read what this fellow wrote.

From what I read, my impression is that he's a so-called good guy. He seems friendly, well put together and happy most of the time. He also likes to think a lot and observe life all around him. He wonders about the nature of life and the universe, but he isn't worried by them. He just finds big questions interesting, just in the same way as he finds going to the movies interesting.

When he comes out, he starts to think about what the movie meant, or whether he understood it, and why the filmmaker did a scene that way. He likes Woody Allen the most of all modern filmmakers. He's one of the most inventive and humorous writers. He has the kind of mind that has thousands of funny ideas dancing through it. The movie *Zelig* is an example. Zelig is like a chameleon who changes shapes and appears in many famous historical events like in Hitler's Third Reich and at Yankee Stadium when Babe Ruth is at bat.

I noticed that Larry is like Woody Allen, in a way. He has ideas in his head that sometimes seem crazy to other people. Some people don't like his "one-liners," but in the family Larry keeps 'em laughing. Dinner at Larry's house is like a three-ring circus. Larry fools around with his brothers, his mother is yelling at them to be quiet and eat and his father is on the phone with clients and partners in his law firm. The television is usually on with the seven o'clock news. The doorbell rings and friends and neighbors drop in for a chat and sometimes stay for dinner. All in all, they are a closely knit family. They work out their problems together. For example, when Larry's grandfather died, they had to figure out what would happen to his grandmother. They talked about it and got her an apartment nearby. Everybody had to say they would visit her at least twice a week to help her and keep her happy. No one thought she should go to an old age home.

Tomorrow I think I'll return the journal to Larry. I'll look him up at school. He's the kind of a guy I'd like to call "friend."

Notes to Larry

- *You've added an introduction that clearly explains why a stranger is reading your journal. You've also written a conclusion, which helps to give your essay a sense of wholeness.*

- *You've added details about Larry's love of movies, and you prove that dinner at home is like a circus. You also show that the family solves problems together, but that discussion probably deserves a separate paragraph.*

- *In the second paragraph you generalize about Larry's personality, but you still fail to show that he's "well put together" (Do you mean physically? Emotionally?) You claim that Larry thinks about big questions. How about some proof? He appears to think only about movies.*

- *Reconsider the section on Zelig. Is such detail necessary? What's the point? Does it add anything to our understanding of Larry?*

- *Sentence variety much improved. Way to go, Larry!*

- *Overall, the paper is still somewhat unfocused. You haven't yet decided whether to concentrate on Larry's personality or on his family.*

Larry's Next Draft

Walking home from school today, I found a notebook on the sidewalk. I took it home and flipped through its pages. It turned out to be a journal that belonged to Larry H. I couldn't resist reading it because he's an interesting person, with a positive, friendly outlook on life. He has a good sense of humor, which is understandable when I saw the kind of family he has. He could hardly survive in such a setting if he took everything too seriously.

Dinner at Larry's house is like a three-ring circus. Larry fools around with his brothers while his mother is yelling at them to be quiet. His father talks on the phone with clients and partners in his law firm. The television is usually on with the seven o'clock news. The doorbell rings and friends and neighbors drop in for a chat and sometimes stay for dinner. Meanwhile, Larry is dropping "one-liners" that send people laughing so they can hardly eat their food.

Sometimes there are serious problems in the family. The laughter stops and everyone gets together to solve the problem. For example, when Larry's grandfather died, they had to figure out what would happen to his grandmother. They talked about it and got her an apartment nearby. Everybody had to say they would visit her at least twice a week to help her and keep her happy. No one thought she should go to an old age home.

I noticed that this two-sided personality also exists in Larry. At times he is funny and inventive. At times he is serious and thoughtful. In a way, he's like Woody Allen's Zelig, a chameleon who changes shape whenever he wants. Larry has ideas that sometimes seem crazy to other people, like when he had a Woody Allen Film Festival at his house. For 24 hours he showed Woody Allen movies to anyone who wanted to see them. He charged 50 cents to get in and gave free admission to anyone who wore an Annie Hall hat or a big rubber nose and glasses like Woody himself.

Woody Allen may be funny, but he's also serious. Larry thinks he's one of the best modern filmmakers. When Larry comes out of seeing a movie he analyzes it, thinking about what the movie meant or whether he understood it, and why the filmmaker shot each scene the way he did. Woody Allen uses big, important ideas like love and death as humor, but Larry wonders about them seriously. He finds it interesting to think about the nature of life and the universe. He isn't worried by them, just interested in thinking about the possibilities.

Tomorrow, I think I'll return Larry's journal. I'll look him up at school. He's the kind of guy I'd like to call "friend." I wonder if he'll be wearing a big rubber nose.

Notes to Larry

- *Much improved.*

- *You've unified the essay by showing that Larry's personality resembles the personality of his family.*

- *Details have added life and color to the portrait of Larry.*

- *Reconsider your presentation of Larry's character traits in the first paragraph. Use examples and anecdotes to show his friendliness and positive disposition—just as you've shown his offbeat sense of humor.*

- *Some of the essay is still a bit awkward. Read your essay aloud, and listen for odd-sounding words and expressions. For example, check the parallelism in the next to last paragraph.*

In this version, Larry seems to have overcome most of the earlier weaknesses in his essay. Of the five comments in the latest note to Larry, only two tell him what to do next. Evidently, he's taken previous suggestions seriously, and his next draft is likely to be his last.

Chuck D's Early Draft

In his essay, Chuck compares riding a bike to living in a competitive world. The idea has merit, but in this early draft Chuck may have been carried away by the uniqueness of his metaphor. Without realizing it, he has presented himself as a rather unappealing and ruthless character. He needs to view his essay with a new set of eyes before going on to write the next draft.

The large brown garage doors of a small split-level home slowly creak open. Out emerges a ten-speed bicycle accompanied by its rider. He checks to make sure his books are secure. He turns and shuts the large doors. As he mounts his bicycle, a shaft of morning sun peeks over the treetops and glistens in his face. He squints and slowly glides out of his driveway. The race has begun.

He moves slowly along the street where he lives. As he approaches his first hill, he casually shifts down to first gear. Slowly but steadily he ascends the hill. As the horizon breaks, he spies a small bicycle about 40 yards away. Like a cat stalking his prey, he increases his speed, legs pumping like pistons. His prey is unaware of his approach. Suddenly, his prey glances back and sees him only a few feet away, but it's too late. Our predator swiftly passes his prey.

Who is this killer on a bicycle? He is me. We are one and the same. Bicycling to school is more than just a means of transportation. It is yet another test of ability. It is a need. It is a psychological contest. Who can get there faster?

Why is this so? I feel that we in the American middle class are brought up to be competitive. When I see another cyclist who I know is going to the same place I am, I feel that I must try to beat him. While I may accomplish nothing by others' standards, in my own mind I have overcome an obstacle. In my mind, to overcome an obstacle is an achievement. I also feel if one achieves the goals which he sets for himself, he will, in his own mind be successful. While beating another bicycle to school is a small achievement, it can give you the feeling, psychologically, of a big achievement, possibly helping to pave the way to bigger and better achievements.

What are the rules which we all must follow? What might happen if we break them? The rules are: Be cool. Never let someone know that you know you are going to pass. Surprise is important. If the person doing the passing were making a lot of noise about it, one of two things could happen: He could forewarn the other person and put him on guard, making it harder for him to pass, or he would cause the person being passed to feel resentful because the person doing the passing would be too showy. Always pass someone without their knowing it. If you are passed, try to regain your ground quickly. If you can't within a reasonable period of time, don't bother. If one did not follow these rules, it would most likely have an adverse effect. If you were to let someone know you know he is passing you, then he would only get that much more joy out of seeing you helpless, or at least unable to compete with him.

As you may or may not have realized, this essay is not about riding to school. This essay is about a world filled with competition. Bicycling is just an example that illustrates just how competitive our world is, or at least how competitive my world is. In high school it has been competitive, and I'm certain it will be the same in college, if not more.

Notes to Chuck

■ *Good, dramatic opening. If possible, build even more tension—the kind you might feel before an important bike race.*

- *The race itself doesn't really begin until the rider spies his competition. Yet, you say it starts when the rider hits the street. Which is more accurate?*

- *Several paragraphs start with questions. The pattern gets repetitious.*

- *The paragraph about rules is long, confusing and repetitive. Do you need all those rules to make your point?*

- *You seem driven by a personal code of ruthlessness, creating the impression that you are selfish, suspicious and sneaky. Do you want a college to think that about you? Would you want to have a friend with those qualities?*

- *Don't explain the point of your essay, as you do in the last paragraph. Let the essay speak for itself. Make the point forcefully enough for the reader to get it without being told.*

- *The basic metaphor of life as a bike race is clear, but you haven't fully explained where else in life you have experienced such intense competition.*

Chuck's Next Draft

The large brown garage door slowly creaks open. Out into the morning sunshine a rider on a ten-speed emerges. He checks his books. Securely mounted. He checks his helmet and the leg of his trousers. All in place. He glides silently down the drive and onto the street, pedaling slowly.

At the first hill he casually shifts down, then slowly but steadily ascends the hill. As the horizon breaks, he spies another cyclist just swinging around the corner onto the boulevard. He increases speed, legs pumping like pistons.

The race is on. He's like a cat, stalking his prey. Slowly the gap between them narrows. His prey is unaware of his approach. Suddenly, his prey glances back and sees him. But it's too late. He's by in a flash, his vanquished victim left in the dust.

Who is this speedster? Who is this cheetah of the road, outracing everyone who crosses his path? It is me. I am the unconquerable one. It's in my blood to race, to overcome, to win, even when it's just the daily ride to school.

Bicycling to school is not just a means of transportation. It is a sport, a contest to see who is fastest. It's a symptom of growing up in the great middle class of America. We have been bred on competition. From Little League to class rank, from college boards to basketball, winning always counts as the only thing that matters. Who is fastest, smartest, tallest, quickest, most popular, strongest, best looking, sexiest, most likely to succeed? Win, win, win says the wind. So, whenever I see another cyclist, I feel that I must try to beat him. It may seem like I have accomplished nothing, but to me it is another achievement, another obstacle overcome in the race of life.

I feel that if you achieve the goals you set for yourself, even the smallest ones, you will be successful in your own mind. While beating another bicyclist to school may accomplish nothing, it satisfies my longing to excel, to feel psychologically that I am better, faster and more ready to face the world.

I don't feel this competitive urge when cycling with a friend. Friends are for getting to know, not for defeating in a race. In friendship there is trust. Neither you nor your friend should feel the other's need to compete. If they feel the need, then friendship terminates, falling as a victim of mutual distrust.

So, the rules of life are like the rules of the bicycle race. Never let someone know you are coming up behind him. A warning will put him on his guard and make the passing more difficult. If you are passed, try to regain ground quickly, but if you can't within a reasonable period, don't try unless you know you can do it. It's better not to let the other person see you in distress, for he'll only get more joy out of seeing you helpless, or at least unable to compete with him. Then he may toy with you, tease you by slowing down and zooming ahead when you think you will pass him.

Long ago, Charles Darwin called it survival of the fittest. That's the way it was and always will be as long as we live in a competitive society.

Notes to Chuck

- *At the start, short sentences and phrases create tension. You've hooked your reader firmly. Good!*

- *You've made yourself much more likeable in this version of the essay.*

- *You show that your competitive urges come from society, not from some dark impulse deep inside you.*

- *The paragraph about friendship adds another dimension to your personality.*

- *In this draft, you make your point clearly—and without specifically telling the reader what it is. Well done!*

- *This essay is almost ready to mail. Read it over carefully for unneeded words and for repetitive phrases and ideas. (For example, in the second sentence, "out" and "emerges" are redundant.)*

After some minor editing Chuck's essay will be complete, and Chuck, being a hard-core competitor, will no doubt send it off confident that it will win him a place in the college of his choice.

APPENDIX B. COMPLETED ESSAYS

When college admissions deans curl up to read a bunch of essays, they look for answers to two key questions about each applicant:

1. What does this essay tell us about the person who wrote it?

2. What does it tell us about how well this person can write?

The second question more or less answers itself when an essay presents a clear and accurate picture of the writer. You won't find many muddled *and* well-written portraits. Therefore, the impression you create rests largely on how vividly you are able to project yourself onto the page.

In this appendix you'll find three college essays. Each, for better or worse, reveals the writer's personality. Before you look at the brief analysis following each essay, decide for yourself whether the essay succeeds. Put yourself in the place of a college admissions officer. What does each essay tell you about its author?

Amy B

Amy entitled her essay "An Evening with . . ." and picked a well-known TV character. She made an inspired selection because the star she chose is not only a popular entertainer but is widely regarded as a show business personality with brains.

> I would like to spend an evening with Benjamin Franklin—Benjamin Franklin Pierce, that is, also known as Hawkeye, the pivotal character of "M*A*S*H," played by Alan Alda. Alda's character portrayal is so real that it is hard to determine where Hawkeye ends and Alan Alda begins. So, I suppose I'd have to set a table for three.
>
> For me, "M*A*S*H" has been a source of entertainment

that seems never to repeat itself. Although I have seen most episodes more than once, I see different things in them each time. Hawkeye possesses not only the ability to make me laugh, but the ability to make me cry as well. "M*A*S*H" is not only a comedy but a statement about man's ability to retain his humanity during war. Hawkeye is the character who, through his sense of humor, his skills as a surgeon, his adherence to decent principles and his loyalties to his friends and his professional oath, serves as the source of strength for his colleagues during the horrors, boredom, fear and pain they face.

I would like to spend an evening with Hawkeye for the same reasons I'd like to spend an evening with a good friend. For sure, it would be a load of laughs! We could bounce ideas around, each of us finishing the thoughts and sentences of the other. It would be easy to talk to Hawkeye because we have so much in common—starting with a sense of humor. Not just any sense of humor, but one that sees the funny or wry side of everyday situations. He sees the funny aspects of others, and he can laugh at himself as well. I share this characteristic; I can be extremely serious, but I know when to laugh, and I don't hesitate to laugh at myself.

In some situations, however, we both use humor as a shield to hide what we're really feeling. In my case it may be merely embarrassment, but in Hawkeye's case it goes much deeper; he uses humor to deny the grubby truth of his situation.

Then there is Hawkeye's ability to see beneath the surface or exterior of people, which I think is basic in understanding others. It is his insight and sensitivity that would make it easy for me to open up to Hawkeye. It is these qualities in myself that make it easy for people to talk to me. Hawkeye has proved himself to be the kind of person to whom one could tell his or her most private thoughts and not have to worry about them being ridiculed or repeated. That's the kind of friend I am, too.

From Alan Alda I would try to gain more insight into the theatrical creative process. I love the theater and have studied acting, performed a few roles and been exposed to professional theatrical people. I know that a career in the theater is not for me, but my affection and feeling for the theater will be a constant interest in my life.

Out of curiosity, I would like to ask Alan Alda, an activist for women's rights, how he felt about Hawkeye's sexist attitudes. On this issue the Hawk and I don't see eye to eye.

For the most part, my discussions with Hawkeye and Alan Alda would go in different directions. Still, I know that both men would ask me what I thought Hawkeye would have to say about life since Korea. After Korea, Hawkeye would have seen the war in Vietnam, the assassinations of the Kennedys and Martin Luther King, Watergate, the war in the Middle East, the decline of the United States as a world power, the drug scene, the deterioration of the environment and nuclear proliferation. He might have had dogs set on him during a civil rights march or seen a son or daughter fired on by the National Guard on a college campus. He, who takes it on himself to disobey evil or irrational orders, would have been sickened by My Lai.

As to what Hawkeye would think about life since Korea, I think he would say, "Well, at least the food's better." Simultaneously with his wisecracking, though, he would have been working to improve the human condition. Hawkeye's later life, after all, was foretold in the final scene of that last episode of "M*A*S*H." Wounded fill the O.R. Gunfire is heard from outside. The surgeons work as usual. The cease-fire is moments away. Suddenly, it is silent outside. "Listen," says Hawkeye. There is no sound to be heard. "What is that?" he asks. "The sound of peace," answers Colonel Potter. "Pass the scalpel," replies Hawkeye.

- *Amy B the person has an original mind and a rich imagination . . . has a strong ego and considerable self-confidence . . . has a playful streak in her . . . takes world events seriously . . . makes it her business to be well-informed . . . takes pride in her social and moral conscience.*

- *Amy B the writer knows how to catch the reader with an appealing opening passage . . . enjoys playing with words . . . appreciates that dialogue can wake up a piece of writing . . . understands how to show her many-sided personality without writing a list . . . sometimes neglects to support general statements with details . . . shows considerable mastery of clear English.*

Peter S

At the start of his essay, Peter addresses the admissions committee directly. Writing the essay, he feels, is like fighting a battle with an unseen enemy.

It is hard for me to believe that the crucial time has arrived when I will leave the protective world of high school and enter another world as a major contestant and participant. Applying to college is my first step as a contestant in a unique kind of battle, one that is fought without blood—only sweat and tears. You, the admissions committee, become the judges. In your heads the decisive victories are won and lost. We, the winners and losers, battle one another only in words. Our minds and souls come to you in a record of scores, letters of recommendation and, perhaps most of all, through this essay. Here you find out about the "me" not revealed in transcripts or through others' words. Each word I write represents another piece to the puzzle of my mind. How I sympathize with you, for some of the pieces may seem confusing or not even part of the puzzle.

Initially, I tried writing an essay that explained how I have been working to improve myself as a person. I grew frustrated with the difficulty of portraying the person I would like you to know, or finding an adequate way to show you my elation over the changes and growth I have experienced, especially since last summer. Now I can picture you sitting there thinking, "Well, here is another kid trying to get into our college by telling us how he has improved as a person." To tell you the truth, that picture makes me somewhat defensive. I know what this war is about: it's essay-eat-essay.

Do you remember when you feared that each word you put down would determine your future? If I had submitted my self-improvement essay, would you have been as deeply moved as I was? Would you have dropped your jaw and danced with excitement as I did when certain events happened to me? Let me try!

I have always wanted to be a more sociable person who, on meeting new people, did not retreat into a shell. Picture me *before:* One day I was stopped at a traffic light when another car pulled alongside. Inside were three of the most gorgeous examples of "pulchritude" I have ever seen. One girl about my age turned toward me. Horror! She was looking straight at me, checking *me* out just as I had done to her! I began to get nervous. Was there egg on my face? Was it April Fools'? Then the most embarrassing thing happened. She waved at me, and what's more amazing, even had the audacity to smile. My pulse went crazy. Was this really happening to me? WOW! I sure would like to meet her. But NO! I shriveled up in my seat. The light changed, and off we went into our own worlds, never to see each other again. So why didn't I wave back? Here was the opportunity I had been waiting for, and what happened? I blew it!

This experience turned out to be a valuable lesson. I began to think, "Is this the person I want to become?"

Many months passed as I sorted out many feelings about myself. During a family vacation in the White Mountains I began to realize that I had to change things that had been part of my personality for so long. I began to experiment with the "new me" during my hikes in the mountains. Each new person I met, I greeted with a hearty "Hello" and a bubbling smile. Not even totally exhausted hikers looked unfavorably at this cheerful, outgoing lad. Then it hit me! This lad was who I really wanted to be.

The new beginning: Back at the hotel I began to worry. I did not want to lose the person whom I wanted to become. I would have to work hard to assume his identity at all times. Trying out my new personality was not always successful, and sometimes the security of my old shell seemed very inviting. But then, *success!*

I had always wanted a job in the dining room of this hotel. On the morning of our departure, I talked with the maitre d' about the mountains, about the hotel, about the dining room, about myself. No matter. Now, I knew what I was doing. I was communicating more easily, without my previous reserve. I was enjoying myself. More importantly, I *knew* there was no egg on my face! At the end of our conversation, I asked the maitre d' if he would give me a job, and you'd never guess what he said. He said, and I quote, "I would love to have someone with your personality working in my dining room!" Well, I hit the 30-foot ceiling!

After reading this essay, did you? Probably not, for it was difficult to convey my feelings and my thinking. But I hit it. Even if my self-improvement essay did not captivate you, I know that I have, in fact, grown.

I cannot deny the past, nor do I want to. Now I feel ready to do battle. My ammunition will come from within, and any victories, as well as any losses, will be my own. I have waged battle with myself, and I am winning. I am liking who I am. No matter what the outcome of this contest, I will keep on growing and evolving into the person I want to be. I want to hit those 30-foot ceilings again and again!

- *Peter S the person seems a bit unsure of himself at the start . . . grows increasingly self-confident as the essay goes on, as well as in life . . . thinks that he's misunderstood—that people don't see the sensitive, complex person residing inside him . . . has a sense of humor . . . has the capacity to change . . . has the resolve to overcome personal hang-ups . . . wants to succeed . . . is sincere . . . has the courage to reveal his anxiety . . . is blessed with charm and a gentle disposition.*

- *Peter S the writer takes risks with words and ideas . . . knows how to project his personality onto the page . . . can use an appropriate story to make a point and develop an idea . . . focuses on an important personal issue . . . demonstrates overall writing competence . . . uses sentence variety and vivid images . . . gets bogged down in wordiness occasionally . . . knows how to write a strong and memorable conclusion.*

Betsy S

Betsy portrays herself with several brief glimpses into her memory. Although the images are separated by time and space, when taken as a whole, they become a finely crafted, unified self-portrait.

Certain experiences that I've had in my life have helped to shape me, along with all my schooling and all that I've learned from other people, into the person I am today. Some of them, although they may have occurred long ago, are still so vivid to me that I feel that I could shut my eyes and be there in those places again . . . .

I grasp the lifeline with my bronzed little 10-year-old hands and stretch my toes down to touch the cold Maine water. Today is beautiful, the water is calm and glistening. The boat leaves a trail of white bubbles behind it as it glides along. We were up at sunrise, Daddy and I were. At least we were up to meet the lobster boats as they went by and we got the first pick of the morning's catch. I had taken a before-breakfast swim and now my swimsuit hangs from the boom, drying in the wind. I turn my head back, lean under the jib and wave to my dad who sits holding the tiller with his bare foot. My mother sits near him, reading a book, my sister is sunbathing and my little brother is playing with the hermit crabs that we've adopted as pets. My father beckons me back to the cockpit and lets me take the tiller. I stand with my bronzed, proud little 10-year-old face gazing up, over the cabin, off at the horizon. . . .

The tears flow down my face, faster still as I glance at my sister and brother, their faces tearstained too. It seems so ironic to me that, at 11 years old, I am standing in the most beautiful restaurant in New York, in the most elegant dress I've ever owned and I am experiencing the most pain I've ever felt. My father glances over his shoulder at us, even as the ceremony is taking place, and I see the pain in his eyes too. I think of my mother, alone at home, in the huge, new house that he just bought for us. What will she have done when he drops us off tonight? Last weekend she tore up their wedding picture. She's broken some dishes and called him every rotten name right in front of me. Inside I've called him them too. I'm only 11 years old and I'm so confused. I love my parents both so much and I'm not ready to have these feelings. I hardly even know this woman he's marrying . . . .

I wake up, having slept for the shortest 4 hours of my life and I force my eyes open and I crawl to the shower as I shampoo my hair. My brain begins to function again and I think to myself, "Any sane person is going to the beach today, sleeping until noon, and wouldn't think of touching a schoolbook." After my shower, I go back to my room and Lindsey, my roommate from Toronto, and I get dressed in a hurry. Grabbing our books we run down the stairs and out the door of our dorm to walk to breakfast. On the way to the Commons, we begin to meet all our friends. It has become a daily ritual, these past weeks at Andover. First we see the kids from Stevens East and Taylor Hall hiking up the hill. Soon we see Jennifer and Dana coming across the quad from Day Hall. We walk into the Commons, grab some Cap'n Crunch and a glass of O.J. and walk over to join the others at a table. I sit back and listen to everyone. They're complaining about their homework, the lack of sleep, the food, the strict curfews, and chattering about our next trip to Boston, letters from home, the newest couple, and I smile at Lindsey and our looks say to each other, "When have we ever been this happy before?". . .

I stand at the top and lift my face up toward the sun. I take off my sunglasses and lean forward onto my poles. I feel every muscle in my body, every muscle in my legs, my shoulders, my arms . . . . A pacific, white sea lies in front of me. There's not another person around me. I'm skiing better than I ever have before. I'm concentrating on every move as if in slow motion. I feel so close to Heaven and so down to Earth. I feel a remarkable energy, maybe from the sun, maybe from the center of the Earth, flowing through me, making me glow. Everything inside me, in my head, seems to come together and I am whole. I lift my face toward the sun and I can't help but smile as I think to myself, "This is me. This is what I am."

There are so many other examples that I could choose to show who I am, many of them are not vivid images of memorable moments, but everyday parts of my life. I love to walk down the hall at school, talking and joking with almost everyone I pass, teachers and students alike. I love the feeling I get when I tutor someone and I help them to understand a concept that they couldn't quite get on their own. Most of all, I love to sit at the kitchen table and talk with my mother and her fiancé, or to go out with my close friends and laugh and hug and know that we can always lean on each other. I work hard and I play hard. I spend a great deal of time studying my books, but also a lot of time forming relationships with other people. I want all the beauty that life can give . . . all the knowledge, all the love. So I fill up my cup and I drink it in.

■ *Betsy S the person loves life and appreciates its possibilities . . . feels and thinks deeply . . . searches below the surface for the essential meaning of everyday occurrences.*

■ *Betsy S the writer has a rare gift for saying what she thinks and feels . . . has composed an essay that deserves to be read again and again.*

APPENDIX C.
STUDENT CONTRIBUTORS*

Elissa Greenberg Adair, Princeton
Amy Becker, Cornell
Chandra Bendix, M.I.T.
Joel Berkowitz, Penn
Ian Biederman, Northwestern
Mario Bonito, Westchester CC
Deborah Brause, Tufts
Brian Cunnie, Penn
Peter Davis, Johns Hopkins
Roger Denny, Columbia
Teresa DiMagno, SUNY Binghamton
Charles DiMicco, SUNY Albany
Sabrina Eaton, Penn
Susan Epstein, Yale
Lisa Estreich, Harvard
Susan Faulkner, Brown
Ellen Gamerman, Swarthmore
Alicia Grant, SUNY Binghamton
Maria Guarino, Fordham
Alexander Harrington, Columbia
Lawrence Harris, Franklin and Marshall
Eric Hecker, Penn
Elizabeth Humphrey, Fordham
Thomas Mackenzie, University of Colorado
Steven Maddox, Harvard
Jon Martin, Cornell
Sally McCauley, Smith
Pamela Meadow, Penn
David Miles, University of California, Berkeley
Michael Miller, New York University
Tracy Parker, Carleton
James Reilly, Duke
Annette Rogers, Boston U.
Elizabeth Schmidt, University of Michigan
Peter Scotch, Connecticut College
Andrew Smith, Washington U.
Gina Smith, Syracuse
Linda Wiereck, Oberlin

*Several contributors chose to withhold their names or to be listed
under a pseudonymn.

INDEX

About the Author

George Ehrenhaft, a graduate of Columbia College and Ohio State, has taught students how to write successful college application essays for over two decades. At present he is the head of the English Department at Mamaroneck High School. He resides in Katonah, New York.

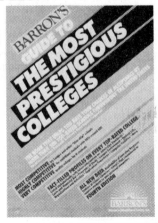

No One Can Build Your Writing Skills Better Than We Can...

Essentials of English $6.95
Can. $9.95
The comprehensive program for effective writing skills.

Essentials of Writing $6.95
Can. $9.95
A companion workbook for the material in *Essentials of English.*

10 Steps in Writing the Research Paper $6.95
Can. 9.95
The easy step-by-step guide for writing research papers. It includes a section on how to avoid plagiarism.

How to Write Themes and Term Papers $6.95 Can. $9.95
The perfect, logical approach to handling theme projects.

The Art of Styling Sentences: 20 Patterns to Success $6.50 Can. $9.95
How to write with flair, imagination and clarity, by imitating 20 sentence patterns and variations.

Writing The Easy Way $8.95
Can. $12.95
The quick and convenient way to enhance writing skills.

Solutions To Your Writing Problems $6.95 Can. $9.95
An easy way to master the essentials of writing style and structure, as well as the transformation of thoughts to words.

BARRON'S EDUCATIONAL SERIES
250 Wireless Boulevard
Hauppauge, New York 11788

In Canada   195 Allstate Parkway
Markham, Ontario L3R 4T8